CREDIT SCORE

How to Navigate the World of Credit and
Effectively Increase Your Credit Score

(Powerful Tips for Legally Improving Your Credit
Score)

Joseph Young

Published by Knowledge Icons

Joseph Young

Credit Score: How to Navigate the World of Credit and Effectively Increase Your Credit Score (Powerful Tips for Legally Improving Your Credit Score)

ISBN 978-1-990084-73-7

Legal & Disclaimer

The information contained in this book is not designed to replace or take the place of any form of medicine or professional medical advice. The information in this book has been provided for educational and entertainment purposes only.

The information contained in this book has been compiled from sources deemed reliable, and it is accurate to the best of the Author's knowledge; however, the Author cannot guarantee its accuracy and validity and cannot be held liable for any errors or omissions. Changes are periodically made to this book. You must consult your doctor or get professional medical advice before using any of the suggested remedies, techniques, or information in this book.

TABLE OF CONTENTS

Introduction

We are speechless when we learn the power that credit can do. Unfortunately, for many people, that is where our lessons on credit management stop. It is at this point of failure, even before we get our first credit card that we begin to fail in our journey.

Adults teach us to pay our bills on time, but they don't teach us how powerful credit can be, how to watch out for the lure of instant gratification or to be wary of identity thieves, unscrupulous scammers, and other dangers that can put our newfound credit reputation in danger.

A young teenager just about to graduate from high school is called into the counselor's office and told that his grant is not sufficient to pay for his college education. A slip of paper is put in front of him, and he is told to sign it. This paper will guarantee that he will get into school the next year. He signs it naively and walks out content that all is right again.

A few years later, he receives a letter stating that his student loan is overdue and he must now pay back to the government what he owes, with interest. He now has a negative mark on his credit report.

A wife of twenty years finally separates from her husband. She wants to get a job and become self-sufficient. She meets her first hurdle when she fills out an application for an apartment, but without an established credit history, she is turned down from one place after another or is forced to pay a huge deposit to secure a safe place to live.

A resourceful businesswoman walks into a bank to open a bank account. She is told that because of a few negative marks on her credit report, the bank will not open an account for her. She is immediately rejected and sent on her way.

These are just a few examples of what can happen when you do not have a fundamental knowledge of credit management. A low credit score can be detrimental to your life in more ways than you can imagine. It involves much more than stopping you from buying that awesome new outfit in the store window. It can also prevent you from having something as basic a need as a bank account or prevent you from finding a means to support yourself.

Regardless of the reason, you might be suffering from poor credit, the natural instinct, when it happens, is that your life almost immediately comes to a halt. You may feel as if you are stuck in the quicksand of negative situations, and it may seem impossible for you to extricate yourself.

Without good credit, you can't get that good job you need to earn enough money to pay your bills. Without a good credit score, you can't find a decent place to live, you can't find a car to get you back and forth to work even if you do, and you can't open a bank account where you can manage your money or put some aside if you need to. Instead, you are forced to go to the highly expensive check cashing services, resort to ulterior means of getting the funds you need, or you're losing precious time away from family and friends just so you can get by and do what you need to do.

Credit is not just a matter of convenience, it is a way of life, and the more you struggle without it, the more you realize what you have lost.

The sad part is losing your credit means you've lost your good reputation in the community. People look at you differently, they respect you less, and they pull away when they know you don't have it. It is very easy to lose your credit reputation, and yet many people have; in fact, millions have. And what's worse, few people are willing to help a person with a low credit score to restore it. It is as if they feel that being associated with someone who I financially irresponsible may somehow rub off on them and taint their own reputation.

Many feel doomed to spend the rest of their lives, struggling to survive against all odds. It feels like everyone is against you no matter what you do. They are not interested in the person but are more focused on those numbers that claim to say all they can about you. This leads you to self-punishment, a sense of self-loathing in some cases, and feeling like you just don't want to try anymore.

Those with a low credit score are the ones that need the most help, and yet they are the ones that are less likely to get it. They don't search for help because society as a whole tells them they are not worthy and few realize that something can be done about it.

Through the pages of this book, we will walk you, step by step through little things you can do that can boost your credit score and get you back into the mainstream of life. You'll learn:

Why we need credit

What is a credit report and how to read it

What is a FICO score and how it is determined

What creditors are looking for when they read your report

Steps you can take to repair your bad credit

And how time can work to your advantage when you have bad credit

If you're struggling with poor credit whether it is because of decisions on your part or something else, we will give you some tools to restore your good name and get you back on track. Most people struggle with a negative mark on their credit from time to time but don't be fooled into thinking there is no way back. Hopefully, by the time you finish reading this book, you'll be back on the road to a viable financial future with a more positive financial image to give to the world.

Here in this book is the answer you've been looking for. A chance to reclaim your life and provide you with everything you need to start again, on the right foot.

There are plenty of books on this subject on the market, thanks again for choosing this one! Every effort was made to ensure it is full of as much useful information as possible, please enjoy!

Chapter 1: Average Credit Score In America: 2017 Facts & Figures

What Is The Average Credit Score In America?

The average credit score in the United States is currently at an all-time high of 695. Though

different scoring models exist, which cause this figure to fluctuate by a few points, most fall

between 660 to 720. This coincides with what the Consumer Financial Protection Bureau

defines as 'prime' - an average score. Approximately 14% of the population has no credit

score whatsoever, and is labeled as credit invisible. As a result, these under banked

individuals will have difficulty obtaining new lines of credit.

In the eyes of lenders, credit scores fall into several buckets, which indicate how risky it may

be to extend credit to an individual. Outside of playing a role in approvals for a loan or credit,

these scores can also impact an individual's lending terms. Perhaps the most important

terms among those are interest rates. The higher an individuals credit score, the lower their

quoted APR will typically be.

Credit scores typically break down in the following manner:

720 or more: Excellent

660 - 719: Average/Fair

620 - 659: Poor

620 or lower: Bad

Though the average credit score has been generally improving, a slight dip occurred around the time of the 2009/2010 recession. A large number of people declaring

bankruptcy or defaulting on their loans would have caused their credit scores to

plummet, which in turn would affect the average.

Average Credit Score By Age

One of the biggest differences in credit scores can be seen among different age groups.

The average FICO score tends to improve with age. The only anomaly occurs in the 30

to 39 age group. These individuals have the largest population of consumers with a

sub-620 credit score. This trend coincides with the financial situation facing many

individuals in their 30s. It is usually around this period in one's life that major

expenses and debt begin to rack up - weddings, first mortgages, etc. A study of

American Credit Card habits revealed that this age group also faces some of the largest amounts of credit card debt.

The other age group whose average credit score skews lower are those below the age

of 30. One contributing factor to this could be the limited access to credit this age

group faces. Following the 2009 CARD Act, it became significantly harder for 18 to 21

year olds to open new credit card accounts. As a result, many young adults do not

begin building up a credit file until later in their life - driving the averages down.

SCORING FOR CREDIT

FTC, OCTOBER 1993

How does a creditor decide whether to lend you money for such things as a new car or a

home mortgage? Many creditors use a system called "credit scoring" to determine whether

you are a good credit risk. Based on how well you score, a creditor may decide to extend credit to you or turn you down. The following questions and answers may help you

understand who gets credit, and why. What is Credit Scoring? Credit scoring is a system used

by some creditors to determine whether to give you a loan or credit card. The creditor may

examine your past credit history to evaluate how promptly you pay your bills and look at

other factors as well, such as the amount of your income, whether you own a home, and how

many years you have worked at your job. A credit scoring system awards points for each

factor that the creditor considers important. Creditors generally offer credit to those

consumers awarded the most points because those points help predict who is most likely to pay back the debt. Why is Credit Scoring Used? In smaller communities, shopkeepers,

bankers, and others who extend credit often knew by word of mouth who paid their debts

and who did not. As some creditors became larger and as the number of their consumer

credit applications grew, these creditors needed to establish more systematic and efficient

methods for evaluating which consumers were good credit risks. Credit scoring is one such

technique. Although smaller creditors still may rely on informal credit evaluations, many

large companies now use formal credit scoring systems. Although no system is perfect, credit

scoring systems can be at least as accurate as informal methods for granting credit -- and often are more so -- because they treat all applicants objectively. How is a Credit Scoring

System Developed? Most credit scoring systems are unique because they are based on a

creditor's individual experiences with customers. To develop a system, a creditor will select a

random sample of its customers and analyze it statistically to identify which characteristics

of those customers could be used to demonstrate creditworthiness. Then, again using

statistical methods, a creditor will weigh each of these factors based on how well each

predicts who would be a good credit risk.

Chapter 2: Improving Your Credit Score In

30 Days

As you have already learned from this book, a higher credit score will mean lower mortgage interest rates, superior credit card offers and better rates of insurance. You should also understand that you do not have to take ages to improve your credit score- a 30 day period is enough to see you massively boost your score and set you on the road toward achieving an excellent score (750+). All you need to do is to know what to do.

Step 1: Carry Out A Comprehensive Diagnosis

The very first step to take is to diagnose the reason for your less-than-perfect score. The easiest way to go about this is to ask yourself the questions below, and to keep track of the "yes" responses that you give.

1: Do you make late payments on your credit accounts?

The most important factor in your score will be your payment history. Late payments will affect your credit score very quickly (and very negatively too). Your monthly installment payment help your score creep up steadily, but all it takes to ruin everything, and move many points back, is one missed payment. Any progress you have made will be reversed quickly. Therefore, if you don't make a payment on or before a due date, simply ensure that you make the payment as fast as you can, as lending institutions have a tendency of waiting for 30 days to lapse (from the payment date) before they report it.

2: Are your credit cards maxed out?

Your credit utilization ratio contributes to your credit score to the same degree as your payment history. By credit utilization, we mean the sum total of credit card debt relative to the total outstanding credit limit. For instance, if all cards are maxed out, this essentially means that your credit utilization is very high. In some circles, this is also called "amounts owed". For instance, if you have a debt of $3,000 and a combined credit limit of $4,000, your utilization ratio is 75%, which is quite poor. You should be looking to keep it at a respectable 25% or below.

3: Do you close your older accounts or perhaps only have accounts that are very new?

The average age of your credit accounts plays a major role. Over time, you will get points in this category, which is why you should not close old accounts. Do not close accounts that you have paid off as well.

4: Do you only use one credit type?

Credit bureaus love to see that you are capable of handling a variety of credit products. For instance, mortgages, student loans and auto loans are all installment loans, which lumps them into one credit category. This is because the balance is fixed. However, a home equity line or credit card will qualify in the revolving credit category. Credit bureaus will hold you in a more favorable light if you have a mix of both, other than only having only one type of credit.

5: Do you often apply for new products of credit?

Every inquiry into your credit or your credit application may cause your score to drop several points.

A soft inquiry, like those made for prequalifying you for various promotional offers, self-checks as well as employer checks will not negatively affect your credit rating. Hard inquiries (those made as a result of applying for new credit), however, will indeed hurt your score. These are the inquiries to limit.

Step 2: Rectification And Strategizing To Lift Your Credit Score

For every "yes" response that you gave, that is at least one credit factor that may be contributing to your weak credit score. The solutions below will help you create a personalized strategy that will improve your score.

1: Check your annual free credit reports for any mistakes present

The Fair Credit Reporting Act, FCRA, requires that each one of the 3 nationwide credit reporting companies: Experian, TransUnion and Equifax, should provide you with a free credit report copy, at your request, every 12 months. The Federal Trade Commission, FTC, which is the US' consumer protection agency is in charge of enforcing the FCRA with respect to the credit reporting companies. All you have to do is to order your free copy from annualcreditreport.com (please note that this is the only authorized website for getting free credit reports- it amalgamates credit scores from the 3 credit reporting companies). You can as well call them on 1-877-322-8228. You will be requested to provide your name, SSN, date of birth and address to verify your identity. The other way through which you can get your free report is by filling the Annual Credit Report Request Form, which you will mail to:

Keep in mind that you won't need to request a report from each credit reporting agency individually, as they all work together to provide free reports through annualcreditreport.com. Also, keep in mind that you can order a report from each company, one at a time or at the same time. You can learn more about getting your free annual credit report from FTC website.

Here is something you need to realize:

It is vital that you go through all three-credit reports:

One mistake too many people make is that they only go through one company's credit report and ignore the other two. They think that they will just read the same things anyway, and as such, there is no need to read them. If you are like this, it is important to understand that there very well may be subtle differences in all 3-credit reports. There is always a chance that you will miss something by ignoring the other two. And in some cases, the details you miss will be the difference between a high credit score and a poor one, and missing out on a credit line that you are trying to secure. Your credit score may take a hit because of uneven reporting present in all 3 reports. For instance, if one of the 3 bureaus does not have any information about your oldest account, the FICO credit score that is derived from this report will likely be lower than for the other two. Therefore, always make sure to go through all 3 credit reports, and thoroughly too. This way, you will miss nothing and you will be able to craft the best credit score improvement strategy, from your base of knowledge.

Some people advice that it is best to request for the credit reports at different times during the year so that you can effectively track your progress. But if you feel it is best to get all your credit reports at the same time, you may want to get statements at any other time of the year so as to track your progress. This will definitely come at a fee.

2: How can you get statements in the mini periods?

NOTE: No other service provides a free credit report other than annualcreditreport.com. Any other company promising to offer a free report will definitely at one point, down the line ask for a payment. If any 'free' credit-monitoring service asks you for your credit card details, that's perhaps a scam!

The best way for you to get credit reports in the mini periods, which is to say outside of the stipulated annual report, is to do so via services that provide the same. You will definitely need to

The best free services for you right now are:

Credit Karma

Nerd Wallet

Credit Sesame

WalletHub

Mint.com

AAA Membership

Some of the best paid services include:

LifeLock

TrustedID

IdentityGuard

Privacy Guard

MyFico

Look for such errors as:

Reports of late payments that are more than 7 years old

Accounts which may not be yours

Accounts that you have paid off that show as unpaid

Accounts which have been discharged in bankruptcy, that are showing as delinquent or having a balance

Tax liens that are paid off, and are over 7 years old

You should also be on the lookout for:

Incorrect names and addresses

Inaccurate employer information

While such personal errors may not have an effect on your credit score, they could be a sign of reporting mistakes, fraud or some other form of foul play.

If you can unearth such errors, the next step to take is to dispute them with the credit bureau. The chapter that follows this one will cover that. However, understand that is your right to have these errors removed in 30 days (45 days tops if the credit bureau needs some more time to review any documents you may have attached.)

2: Enhance your credit utilization to give your credit score a quick boost

There are 2 ways that you can go about this and if you can apply them easily, your credit score will get bumped up in as little as 30 days. These ways are-

-Make a huge payment to offset your credit card debt

The thing is; your credit score will automatically increase when your credit card balances go down. More precisely, if you pay off a credit card that is maxed out, you can actually give your score a positive boost by as much as 100 points within 30 days. Also, in truth, the specific dollar values don't really matter. What matters is the debt amount that you carry, when expressed as a percentage of the amount of credit that you are allowed.

-Increase your credit limit without necessarily having an increase in your debt:

For instance, if you have a balance of $1,500 with a credit limit of $3,000, your ratio sits at 50%. This is not good. However, if the issuer increases the credit limit to say $6000, this essentially allows you to bring down your credit utilization rate to 25%. This is quite respectable, and you have done this without even paying anything to lower your account balance. However, if you are going to attempt to use this strategy, make sure you already have good credit.

3: If you have really poor credit, use different credit account types

This will help to improve your score quickly.

You may have made a few bad financial decisions or had poor management in the past and your credit score has suffered for it. You may also have significant trouble qualifying for a traditional credit card that you can then use to build credit.

In this case, you may want to get a secured credit card to start you on your way to a good track record of paying off debt in good time.

A secured credit card will necessitate a refundable security deposit, which you have to pay. The issuer of the card uses this amount as security/collateral. Basically, what you are doing is backing up your credit limit using your secured credit card using the deposit amount. Once this is done, combine responsible future actions with the other strategies in this chapter.

Next, we will discuss what you should do with the errors that you may find in your credit report.

Chapter 3: Credit Limits And Why They're

Important

I Stopped Maxing Out My Credit Cards

You may not be aware that using your credit card each month until you've almost hit your credit limit may very well be keeping your FICO score low and your credit risk high.

Anyone in a position to give you credit wants to know that you are not living beyond your means or at the very edge of your means.

They will look at how much credit you have available to you, and if you are consistently reaching the limit on your credit cards, they will think that there's a high risk that you may default on one or more of your bills. What if there's an emergency and you need access to emergency money, which your credit cards can provide? There won't be room on any of your credit cards for an emergency situation. Given all of these reasons: Credit denied.

When my credit started to improve and I was approved for my first credit card, I used it for everything in order to obtain reward points that were offered by my credit card company. (I could exchange whose points for other items like gift cards or plane tickets.) I paid off the card in full every single month and was never late on any of my payments.

Given my great track record with this card, I couldn't understand why I couldn't get a limit increase and I was still being denied other forms of credit.

What I didn't know was that by charging to my card's limit every month, I was still seen as a high-risk person to grant credit to.

In other words, my credit utilization ratio or credit-limit-to-debt ratio was very high. This is the percentage (ratio) of debt someone has compared to the available credit that person has. You can find out what your credit utilization ratio is by taking your total credit card balances and dividing that by your total credit card limits.

If I had a credit card with a limit of $1200 and had $1100 of debt charged to that card, my credit utilization ratio would be 92%. (1100 divided by 1200 is .92) This is much too high. Credit cards companies like to see credit utilization ratios as low as possible and never more than 30%. As of the writing of this book, my credit utilization ratio is 6%.

When I learned how important this percentage was, I stopped using that card for most of my expenses which left a lot of unused credit on my credit card each month. The credit card company saw this as a good thing, and I saw an almost immediate increase in my credit rating.

Keeping my balances low on my credit cards and any other revolving lines of credit greatly improved my credit rating.

Chapter 4: How Many Cards

What's tricky about this factor is that it could affect your credit either way. One person may close a credit card and their score goes up, another could do the same and their score goes down. The last thing a creditor wants to see is ten open credit cards on a report. The problem with having a lot of open cards is if they were to close half their cards, they may be worse off than had they just left them all open. Ideally it's good to have three cards that are used, each maintaining a revolving balance that is paid on time. But don't hit the panic button if you already have too many cards. The best way to handle this type of situation is to sit down with each card and see what they offer your report.

How to Improve: When determining if some cards should be closed, look at what each card offers you. Keep in consideration both things you benefit from and things your credit report benefits from. For example, a card with a lower APR or better reward system benefits you more. While on the other hand a card that has been opened a long time or has a high credit limit benefit your credit report. Ideally keep cards that meet both needs, but in the long run the cards that benefit your credit report should be kept.

Keep in Mind: Before closing any cards; get the rest of your credit in order saving this for last. That way, it will be easier to see how much it is pulling or raising your score, and give you a better idea if closing cards will benefit your credit.

Balances That Default

This could be a credit card that was charged off or even a car that was repossessed. Any debt that you stop paying will remain on your credit report for eight years, and will be negatively impact your credit the entire time. Once the debt is paid off, there still will be a mark that it defaulted, but will be less significant after the debt is paid. Some people will find when they attempt to get

31

a home loan that the first thing they do is have you pay any debts that were defaulted.

How to Improve: If there's any debt that you stopped paying, the first step is to contact who currently owns that debt and see what they can do for you. In most cases when a collection agency buys defaulted debt, it's for pennies on the dollar. What this means to you is that the collection agency may be willing to settle for less than what is owed.

Keep in Mind: That whenever a debt defaults it will remain on your credit for seven years from the time it went delinquent. If the debt is showing after seven years (which can happen when a collection agency buys your debt) then dispute the charge with the credit bureau to get the debt removed.

Inquiries

An inquiry refers to any time your report is pulled for viewing. It could be when your credit is ran for applying for a new card, car loan, or viewing it yourself. It's vital to know when an inquiry will occur to avoid it happening unnecessarily. A big cause is every time you call a credit card company and ask for a credit limit increase. In the end they may decline you and all that was managed was a slightly worse score. Some credit card companies do offer a service that allows you to view your credit report without placing an inquiry; these services come in very handy when you want look at your report without consequence.

How to Improve: The best way to maintain a low inquiry count is to only apply for credit or view your report when it's needed. Whether it's a credit card or not, always ask if an action will place an inquiry on your report.

Keep in Mind: That it is impossible to get around all inquiries, if you're looking to use your credit then inquiries are going to happen.

Debt to Income ratio

 When you apply for a credit card they will almost always ask how much your current household income is. Now before you get excited and just write down a million dollars expecting the highest limit offered, realize that what will not lie about how much you make is your credit report. It's easy to determine about what someone makes from their debt history. Because after all, someone that makes a million dollars won't have a 100K mortgage they have been paying off for five years. For those of you saying to yourself there is nothing on your report, they can just as easily ask for a copy of a pay stub before processing your application any further.

 How to Improve: The best way to handle household income is just to be honest, after all you should just be intending on using a portion of your limit anyways.

Keep in Mind: That depending on your income and credit, your credit limit may be set very low to start, but just remember that as your credit improves, your limits will automatically increase.

Debt increase/Decrease

This may not mean much to someone new to credit, but how your debt has went up or down is a strong sign of how well financially someone is doing. This could go both ways; someone that jumped in debt drastically will be seen as a risk. Someone who had high debt and it was abruptly paid off will be questioned what happened or caused the drastic pay off. If they find it was due to a large sum of cash awarded, they may be less apt to approve the credit.

How to Improve: If following the other factors about where balances should be compared to limits, as your credit improves and your limits go up; the balances will soon follow. The key here is consistency. Regardless which way the debt is going, as long as it is slow and steady helps ease concerns about its fluctuation.

Keep in Mind: Red flags go up for any creditor when the debt has drastically changed in the past.

All these reasons combined (along with others) come together to form your report, and ultimately your score. It can seem very overwhelming, but it is important to understand how many factors are encompassed. I have heard too many people that make all their payments on time and cannot understand why they are denied.

The Mind Set of Credit

Whether you have yet to apply or have been in credit your whole life, to get into the right mindset is only going to improve your score and financial life regardless of what it looks like now. Granted, if you just filed for Bankruptcy yesterday, it may just take a little longer to show.

The best way to develop credit habits is to think of yourself on a "credit" diet. Just like a diet, by sticking to your goals long term will grant you success. It's okay to cheat every so often, maybe making a purchase here or there that you want. The problem is when this becomes constant or the whole credit diet gets thrown out the window. And just like a diet, depending on how in shape your credit is now will give you an idea of how long for it to get in shape. If you are in the habit of living off your credit cards, sit down and crunch numbers to see if you can find a budget that will get the balance going in the right direction. If there seems to be no way possible, then it's time to contact a debt consolidation agency to help get your credit in order. They are in a unique position as they can usually get lower interest rates through arrangements they have with creditors. As helpful as consolidation companies can be, they will make you close your cards and have a negative impact on your credit.

When some people think of credit they think of constant bills draining their money. Others are thinking of all the sweet material things they can be getting. The thing to understand is that people with amazing credit still could be thinking about all the things they want to buy. The difference is they do it responsibly and at an interest rate that costs them minimal money. Let's say two people want to buy the same car, and this car costs $10,000.

The first person doesn't have a strong credit score and ends up paying 300 a month for their car payment. The second person ends up only paying 150 dollars a month. This goes to show that the worse your credit, the worse your interest rate, the more you're paying. Now compound this example to everything dealing with credit from a house to a card. I can still remember when I turned on my utilities they ran a credit check to determine if a 150 deposit was needed. At the time I was broke from moving and could not afford the deposit. You may say 150 dollars isn't much, but it is just one example. All these things add together, and that total may not always be so small.

Chapter 5: How To Fix Your Credit

In the previous chapter, we read about what it takes for you to have a bad credit score and the various factors that can determine it. In this chapter, we look at the best ways in which you can better that score and repair your credit in a fast and efficient manner.

Pay off debt

The very first thing that you have to do to better your score is to pay off all the debt. This is, in fact, the best way for you to better your score. As soon as you come into money, decide to repay your debts, so that it will have a positive impact on your credit report.

You can repay your debt in one of the following two ways:

Avalanche

Under the avalanche method, you start by paying off the debt that has the highest interest rate attached to it or the highest amount of debt that is present in your account. Say you have two debts of 10,000$ and 7,000$, then you pay off the 10,000$ and then move to the 7,000$ debt. This method will have an immediate and large bearing on your credit report and one that will shoot up your credit score.

Snowball

This method is the opposite of the above method as it will allow you to go for the low interest payments first and then move to the high rates. That way, you keep yourself interested in the process and it will hook you up with the habit of repaying all your debts. This is best done when you have only a little money with you, which is enough to help you pay off a small debt.

You can choose the method that suits you the best. Ideally, you can opt for the first method, as it will help take off a lot of weight from your shoulders in one go.

Check with creditors

The next best thing that you can do is check with your creditors and see if they will give you a little more time to repay your debt and not include it in your credit report. Ask them if they will not mention it as a late payment, as it will look bad on your score. Once it is mentioned, it will be very difficult for it to be erased and so, you must try and persuade them to listen to you and give you a chance.

But remember that this might work just once and your creditor might not be generous always. And even after giving you time you don't pay, then it will look very bad on your part.

Avoid using a credit card

When you have a bad credit score, you will make it worse by using your credit card. You will already have a low credit and if you add to it by making more purchases then it will up your debt. So if you have a bad score, then try your best to not use your credit card at all. If you need to make a purchase then imply pay by cash or if you have someone then make them use their card to buy it for you. You can keep your cards hidden, until such time that you clear all your debts.

Opt for a secured credit card

If you feel that you will not be able to stay away from your credit card and will have the urge to use it every now and then, then you can opt for a secured credit card. A secured credit card is something that your bank will issue and is more or less like a debit card. It will issue a small limit like say 500$, which you will have to pay first and then you can draw from it using your card. That way, it will not show badly on your credit score and you will not have a large sum to pay as interest.

Life insurance borrowings

The next thing you can do is to borrow some credit against your life insurance. This is best done as a last resort when you have no plans of filing bankruptcy. You can call your insurer and tell him that you will be borrowing a certain sum. This sum will be yours itself but will be deducted from your insurance policy. By doing this, you will at least have some peace of mind and not worry about your debts. You can also borrow this some and then return it back with interest, so that it does not affect your policy and ultimately, you will be able to claim the full sum of money from you insurance company.

Have another account

This step will help you in a big way. When you have a bad credit score, it will look odd if you open up another account but it will be necessary. Another account will allow you to have one for your expenses and one savings account, where you can transfer a certain sum of money on a monthly basis. That way, you will be able to buy what you need and also have an account where you are saving money for yourself and can use it to pay off your debts and repair your bad credit. Split your pay cheque in such a way that the first budget account gets only 10% and the rest 90% goes to the second account.

Borrow from family

The next step can be to seek the help of family members. You can take your parents, siblings, cousins; uncles etc. help and repay all the debts so that you don't get a bad credit score. You can promise to repay them with or without an interest. That way, you will not have to pay hefty interest like you would have to with a bank loan or not have to pay it at all if the sum you borrowed is not that big.

Take help

If you are finding it difficult to make the decisions by yourself and not knowing how to go about with the process, then you can enlist the help of a chartered accountant friend or a banker friend to help guide you. You can also ask a wise person, who has been in a similar situation, and ask them to give you advice.

Get small cards

Sometimes, it is best that you get multiple cards instead of just your credit cards. These cards can be gas station cards, grocery store cards etc. By repaying these, you will be able to positively contribute towards your credit report and up your credit score. Just make sure that you don't buy cards with huge values and take those with nominal values. This will have an immediate impact on your score and month after month, it will keep getting better.

Update

The last step is for you to update your new score. Once you think you have repaid a lot of your debt, you can check your credit report. You will also be able to correct any mistakes from it and have a clean report. You can get it done through one of the credit agencies that were mentioned in chapter 1.

Looking at your repaired credit, you will have better days ahead of you where you will not have to worry about bad credit scores and not being able to live a good life.

Chapter 6: Overcome The Spending Habit

If human beings were rational this chapter might only be six words long:

Don't buy what you don't need.

But we are not rational and the pressures to spend beyond our means come at us hard from all angles. We strive to keep up with those around us. We fall prey to our own impulses. Increasingly sophisticated marketing efforts bombard us day in and day out. In times of economic trouble even our government pleads with us to spend.

Any nagging thread of reason is easily overcome by these pressures and we struggle as a result. Who really has control here? How do they become such a deciding factor in our financial lives?

The answers are found deep inside us.

Believe it or not 'keeping up with the Kardashians' is a survival instinct. In order to make certain that we are desirable, which is fundamental to the human condition, we need a yardstick, a measurement tool. Our neighbors, our co-workers and even the most ridiculous entertainment personalities are that yardstick. As summed up by Hill and Buss in The Evolutionary Psychology of Envy, "people's feelings of success and failure at life's pursuits are formed by comparing their own performances to those of others."

While the envy response is understandable and even important in many aspects of human endeavor, without sufficient control it can lead to devastating ends. Excessive mortgages, overuse of credit cards, and buying for status are all precursors to financial hardship. Envy can also lead to impulse buying, especially in those who harbor feelings of deficiency.

Impulse buying has been studied extensively. The trigger to buy is neurological. Acquiring something we desire and the anticipation of it both release dopamine, a compound associated with pleasure and motivation that encourages us to pursue activities we enjoy.

While there is nothing inherently wrong with the impulse, occasionally those 'activities we enjoy' are unhealthy. Yet we are driven to pursue them nonetheless because, though we hate to admit it, we are hardwired more for pleasure than for reason. Not surprisingly, dopamine is related to many addictions. Impulse buying itself can be an addiction with all the inherent dangers.

The frustration in all this is that even when we know we are being pushed to act by the chemicals in our brain, overcoming their influence is extremely hard work. Imagine how hard it is for the vast majority who are wholly unaware of this unseen master?

It is enlightening that when you research dopamine you find many of the studies being consumed by the marketing industry. Learning how to best take advantage of our propensity for pleasure can make for powerful marketing strategies.

We can debate the ethics of this at another time, however, given that marketing targets our unconscious triggers, if we seek to control our own decisions it is critical that we take steps to defend ourselves against both internal and external influence. But how?

Knowledge and Habits are the best defense.

In order to understand the extent of the problem in our lives, we have to start by establishing where we are.

Until we consciously acknowledge the full extent of our buying habits, we are slave to our impulses.

To break free, begin by performing a thorough expense review, an objective and detailed analysis of past expenses. Since impulse buying is largely 'unreasoned' it is also largely 'unconscious'. As a result, if we simply reflect on our buying habits we will often ignore or significantly diminish the impact these purchases have on our monthly outlay. Thankfully, between online banking and credit card statements, we have excellent data to help keep this process objective. The real challenge is mustering the courage to come to the table in the first place.

The greatest obstacle to being financially honest with ourselves is fear of judgment, both from others and from ourselves. Until we set aside that fear we cannot move forward.

The following commitment statement was drafted for couples undertaking this process. It can be equally meaningful for individuals who judge themselves harshly:

"This is a not a time for blame. This is not a place to judge. We do this to learn and to grow. We do this to build a better future together.
We do this to strengthen our life together."

Once you are able to come to the table, the process is simple. Take every purchase, every bill, every cash withdrawal for the past three months and tag them individually using the following categories:

Mandatory expenses – food, housing, essential transportation, utilities, insurance, etc. These are amounts required to function, which must be paid each and every month without question.

Savings – Saving is an essential habit of financial empowerment. If you currently have no regular amounts being saved each month, don't worry, you are not alone. But changing this pattern will be a dramatic leap toward a more positive financial future.

Carefully considered desires – These are expenditures that, though not key to your survival, are crucial to maintain or create the quality of life you expect. These might include internet, cell phone, recreational activities, vacations, etc.

Non-crucial desires – These are habitual expenses that we often think of as crucial though, if we are honest, we find they are not. These are unique to every household and individual. For some, pet-grooming is crucial, for others not so much. Some consider record collecting fundamental to their lifestyle, for others it's a hobby of diminishing interest. Identifying and eliminating non-crucial desires can make a significant reduction in the amount you spend each month.

Unnecessary Expenses and Unnecessary Fees are the next two. These are the 'easy to identify' expenses you will eliminate in future months.

Personal Investment – This refers to any amounts you are investing toward your own future and long term goals. (We will discuss goal setting in greater detail in chapter 11.) Personal investment is a category often overlooked, especially by those struggling to make ends meet. Developing a strategy to change that will be covered in future chapters.

Going through this process will provide a very clear picture of your spending habits. Don't be surprised if you are discomforted by the results. You will find yourself justifying your lattes and late fees. This is natural, but know that these justifications do not emanate from your rational mind. Ignore them. View the results without judgment as a picture from your past. Your future does not have to look the same.

The power in this process is identifying what past habits to be on the watch for. Our buying habits are driven by our subconscious. They will put us to the test.

Some other simple and direct tips to help build positive habits include:

Put One Thing Back – Before going through the register, look through your basket. At least one item is unnecessary or overpriced. Set it aside.

Mirror Saving – When pulling cash from an ATM, transfer the same amount to savings. This action helps build the habit of saving and reduces the visible balance of your checking account.

Discretionary Cash – You might feel that eliminating the option to buy something unexpected, and yes even unnecessary, is a form of torture. That's fine. Go crazy!

But budget for it. Give yourself a set amount of discretionary cash to use each month however you'd like. But when you're out, you're out.

POS (point of sale) reminder stickers — Overwhelmingly, we use credit and debit cards for our regular purchases. These are a wonderful convenience. However, when paying with plastic we have very little attachment to the expense. We don't recognize the 'loss' that our purchase represents. A simple sticker on the front of your card is a quick reminder when you need it most.

POS reminder stickers are available at:**www.FinancialEmpowermentServices. com/credit-friendly/**

Whatever you can put in place to help insure your purchases remain intentional will serve you well in the end.

The struggle to avoid unnecessary expenses is a struggle against culture, against the forces of economics, even against ourselves. Nonetheless, it is a struggle that can be won; that must be won. And it brings us that much closer to financial empowerment and better credit when we do.

Recommendations to help you **Overcome the Spending Habit:**

1. Do a thorough and objective expense review. Learn the full extent of your buying habits.

2. Be on the watch for internal and external spending pressures. Stay strong!

3. Build new habits that limit spending and strengthen saving.

Chapter 7: Building Business Credit

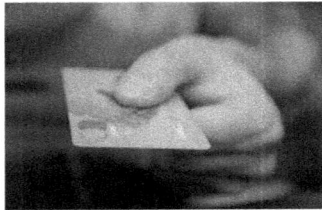

Approximately 45 percent of all small businesses who are turned down for a loan have bad credit to blame, according to the Federal Reserve Banks of Philadelphia, Cleveland, Atlanta and New York. A robust credit profile for your business doesn't just make it easier to get a loan, it will also make it easier for your business to attract new customers. This is because, unlike with your personal credit report, anyone including potential suppliers, partners and customers can all see the credit report of your business at any time. With this fact in mind, it should be clear that if you own a small business, you will want to do everything in your power to improve its credit as quickly as possible and keep it clean as well.

Know your current score: While you are already familiar with Equifax and Experian, when it comes to keeping tabs on your business credit score you are also going to need to familiarize yourself with the Dun & Bradstreet credit bureau. Unfortunately, while determining your personal credit score is relatively straightforward, all three bureaus use a different means of determining business credit scores as well as asking various lenders for differing types of data. This will sometimes work to your advantage, however as Dun & Bradstreet lets business owners update their basic business details and also upload financial data. Even better complete portfolios actually improving overall credit scores.

Set up trade lines: Assuming you purchase materials from third-party vendors, doing so in the right way can help you to improve your business' credit. Assuming you have been working with a given vendor for some time, it is likely that they would be willing to extend you trade credit for the things you purchase most often. Trade credit simply means that you will be able to pay a predetermined number of weeks, or even just days, after you have received the latest shipment of inventory. Once you set up this type of relationship it is then easy to ask the supplier to report your payments to the relevant credit bureaus.

You will want to try your hardest to establish at least three of these types of relationships as doing so will allow you to get what is known as a Paydex score through Dun & Bradstreet which is a measure of your successful payment history. Even if you form relationships with smaller vendors who don't typically report details, by listing them on your account as trade references the bureau will then follow up with them to generate your score.

Be prompt with payments: Just like with your personal finances, paying creditors on time is a crucial part of building your business credit successfully. If you are looking to get the best Paydex score from Dun & Bradstreet you are going to need to go above and beyond and make all your payments early, no exceptions. Additionally, the longer your credit history the better so the sooner you can start forming these relationships the better it will be for your score.

Borrow from the right lenders: While having a loan and paying it on time can help to boost your business' credit score, this will only be the case if the lender you choose reports to the bureaus which is far from guaranteed. Do your homework and make sure that your fiscal responsibility is helping you out as much as possible when you do get a loan. Most banks will report to the bureaus as do the online lenders including BlueVine, Kabbage, Funding Circle Fundation,

Lending Club and OnDeck. Fundbox, Lighter Captial, SmarBiz and most merchant cash advance companies do not. If you are using business credit cards, strive to keep your credit utilization under 20 percent for the best results.

Be aware of your public records: Just like your business credit report, your public records can also be seen by anyone which means you are going to want to do your best to stay on the right side the law. Not only will negative public records affect your business credit score, they will affect the way the public perceives your business as well.

Stop collectors fast.

While it is always going to be a better choice to deal with creditors directly rather than waiting for a debt to reach collections, if it does reach this point it is important to keep in mind that you still have options thanks to what is known as the Fair Debt Collection Practices act.

Ask for details in writing: Within 5 days of making contact, a debt collector is obligated to send you a written notice outlining the amount of money you owe, who you owe it to and how to dispute the claim. Most debt collectors won't do this automatically, however which means the first contact you have with them should include asking for this information and nothing else. The goal of the debt collector is to force you to confirm that you will pay the debt or make a payment, and not having all of the details in front of you can make it easy to say the wrong thing and wave many of your rights without even realizing it. What's more, asking for a copy of the details will prevent them from contacting you again until you have received them, giving you some time to get your defenses together if you have been caught off guard.

Dispute the claim: Once you have received the details of the claim in writing, the next thing you are going to want to do is to dispute the claim using the methods discussed in previous chapters, regardless of whether or not you believe you owe the money in question. This will put the onus on the collection agency to verify the debt, which is far from a sure thing even on debts that you do owe. You have 30 days to send this letter from the date you received the details which means that using certified mail is key. Be sure to ask for a delivery receipt as nine times out of ten the collections agency will deny they received your request. Once you send this letter and notify the collection agency of this fact, they cannot contact you again until the debt has been verified. They also have to stop all reporting activity, make sure you demand this in the letter.

Keep track of everything: As discussed previously, debt collectors are limited in how they can approach you but, in most cases, will try and skirt these restrictions as much as possible in an effort to get you to agree to pay the debt or set up a payment plan. As such, it is in your best interest to take detailed notes every time you speak with them and keep anything they send you so you can look it over for violations at a later date.

Illegal activities not previously covered include speaking to anyone but you or your representation about the debt, using abusive language, misrepresenting the amount of the debt of making false claims about legal action, seizing property or garnishing wages if they don't intend to actually follow through. If they do any of these things, then the issue of the amount of debt you owe will essentially become moot as you will be able to take legal action against them and even the threat of doing so will often be enough for them to forgive some or all of your debt entirely. Be sure not to mention that you are keeping track of your conversations as this will cause them to be on their best behavior and decrease your potential for leverage.

Speak as little as possible: Everything that a debt collector says is for the purpose of collecting on the debt which means that the less you say, the less they have to use against you. Remember, regardless of what they may say up front, they are never really your friend, nor do they have your best interests at heart. They work on commission which means the more they get from you the more they will make. Never commit to anything, never agree that you owe the amount in question, always mention that you are considering bankruptcy and discuss payment options only if you intend to follow through. If they determine that you are unlikely to pay, and the amount owed is less than $2,500, they may give up and consider you more trouble than you are worth. While the debt will remain on your credit report for the next seven years, it might be worth it, depending on your current financial situation.

Be aware of time limits: Once you receive the details from the collection agency, you will need to look into the timeframe which they have to collect on the debt based on where you live (between three and six years in most cases). Once this period of time has passed they can no longer take legal action against you. It is important to be aware of these limits as if you make a payment after this period of time, some states will allow the clock to be reset, the same can be said for acknowledging you owe the debt or for signing up for a repayment plan.

Chapter 8: How You Can Challenge Bad Credit Even If It Is Your Own Bad Credit

First, you might in fact be very tempted to choose an attorney or financial expert to help fix your bad credit. However, this is not always a good idea. Yes, it may seem a fantastic way to help you change your bad credit around within a short time, but this might not be the best option for you personally.

The costs for a start can be too much and you can easily change your credit by yourself. Credit scores do not change overnight; it can take time, hopefully not years, but a little time in order to improve. There are companies who say they can change the credit around within a day and that just is not going to happen.

It takes a lot of work to change bad credit. There are going to be time when you need to challenge some of the bad credit on your credit report and while companies can handle this, it's much better for you to do this yourself. Dealing with a third party can often get confusing and talking to the creditors face to face yourself seems much more satisfying.

So how can you challenge bad credit on your credit report?

Well, firstly, you need to get a hold of your credit report. In fact, you could be entitled to a free credit report. There are many ways to obtain a free credit report, so do not be afraid to ask for yours!

You can get your free report from Trans Union, Equifax or Experian and once you receive your report, you should check over it entirely.

This means checking precisely and carefully, and at times, that means going over it with a fine toothcomb twenty times. If you do happen to spot bad items on the report that you do not like, you can take a good note of it.

Remember, though, before you go charging in like a bull in a china shop, check to see if the negative report has been removed from the time you checked the report and a few weeks later. Most credit bureaus update the data they have every so often so the chances are it could be gone within a few weeks.

File a Dispute Online

If you want to challenge a bad report on your credit report, then you could do so online. You will have to file a dispute on the web at a credit bureau website. You will need to fill out a form on the website and you need to say about which negative report or reports you want to dispute. You also need to give the reasons why you want to dispute it as well.

Once you have done so, make a copy for yourself just for your records. However, the amount of time in which it takes a credit bureau to respond can vary. It might be twenty-four hours or weeks so be patient.

If you find a month, or thirty days have passed and there have been no signs of communication from the credit bureau, call and ask what is going on. Most of the time, you will hear back from them.

It could take thirty days remember so wait until that time period is over because the bureau have to investigate the dispute. If they agree with you, they also need to make the appropriate corrections as well so it takes time. If you have been successful however, you will receive a new credit report.

If you are not happy with the decision, call and ask the creditor about the bad report. Remember, the credit bureaus can only go by the information given on the creditors data so do not blame them if the decision does not go your way. There might be an error on the creditor's part.

If there have been bad credit on your part, then you could ask the creditor if they could remove it. This way it helps your credit in the end.

However, even if you want to dispute bad credit – even if it is yours – you can!

Can You Dispute Anything Even If it is Correct?

Anyone can dispute anything on his or her credit reports. Let us not get into the whole morality thing because some people will dispute everything and some will dispute nothing, it is up to everyone's own individual choice.

You have the right to have every single piece of information on your credit report to be one hundred percent accurate. You will want verifiable information on there too! So yes, you can dispute any piece of information contained on your credit report.

How Can You File A Dispute Without Going Online?

First of all, if you want to file a dispute, you need to create a very nice, polite but thorough letter. You should word the letter very carefully and say you would like a piece of information verified and if that information cannot be verified, remove it from the report.

Do not say that accurate information should be removed from the report; instead, say you want something to be verified. The credit bureau will then get in contact with the lender and will either get the information verified or unverified.

Can You Re-Dispute Something?

Once you dispute something on your credit report, you can in fact re-dispute it. You will go through another dispute form and the reasons why you want to dispute it again. However, the results could be the exact same, but if you were to contact the lender and talk to them, you might be able to win the dispute.

Sometimes, the credit bureau might not go through another dispute claim so you need to be wary of that.

What You Need To Remember

First, your credit reports are very important because it contains all of your important information on it. It has information such as your previous address's, your finances and even how you pay your bills at the end of each month! It also contains information about whether or not you have ever filed for bankruptcy or even been sued as well as much more information.

Remember, all of the information on your credit report can affect whether you are able to take on a loan in the future. It can also determine how much money you can borrow and how you have to repay the money back as well. This is why it is important to have only accurate up to date and of course complete information contained on it.

Any misinformation can work against you even if it is only a year old, it can go against you when it comes to making major purchases. If you wanted to purchase a car or mortgage then the amount you could borrow could go against you; what is more, if your credit was in a terrible state, you might not even be able to purchase a home at all!

That is why it is important to keep the information on your credit report up to date.

Chapter 9: How To Establish Your Credit

If you've never applied for a loan or a credit card in the past, the process in which to obtain these types of financial securities might seem foreign to you. What's more, many people don't even know where to begin in terms of how to gain access to owning a credit card. First, it's important to understand that there is research that's required before applying for a credit card. Your credit score is the most important factor when applying for a credit card because many types of cards exist that will not accept customers who have credit scores below a certain level. For example, some fancy American Express credit cards require that you pay an annual fee in exchange for using their services, and their customers must have credit scores between 750 and 850.

Due to this fact, when you're first starting out establishing credit it's important to only apply for credit cards that are known as more "beginner" cards. These cards accept people with lower credit scores. A great example of a credit card that's geared more towards people who are just starting to build their credit is the Discover It card. Be sure to look into this type of card if you think opening an account with Discover could be beneficial to your credit building goals. If you have absolutely no credit at all, you may not qualify for even a beginner card such as Discover It. Don't panic. There are options that exist for a person with absolutely no credit to grow their credit history. If there were no options for beginners, how else would anyone be able to grow their credit? Here we will look at the steps that are necessary when taking your credit from nonexistent to something stable and reliable.

Step 1: Apply for a Secured Credit Card

The only way in which a secure and unsecured credit card differ is in the fact that a secured credit card requires a down payment. The down payment for a secure card ranges between three hundred to five hundred dollars. This can explain the name "secured" credit card, because the money that you put down serves as a security deposit on your loan. By giving the credit company a down payment, you are promising them that you will repay the funds that you borrow, because if you don't you will lose the money that you originally gave them. Your activity with this card will serve to grow your credit, as long as you make your payments on time, of course. Be sure to not confuse a debit card from a secured credit card. Your debit card history is not reflected on your credit score.

Step 2: Charge Only What Can Be Paid Back Fully

It's smart to start small when you are first establishing your credit. In conjunction with this, it's an equally smart idea to only make payments with your credit card when you know that you will be able to pay this money back in full at the end of the month. The primary way in which credit card companies make their money is by charging interest each month on any borrowed money that is outstanding in your account at the end of the month. For example, if you only buy one pair of shoes with your credit card for the month and they cost $75.00, it would be in your best interest to pay the credit card company the full $75.00 at the end of the month. Of course, you have the option of only paying $30.00 or whatever other amount you wish to pay, but the remaining amount of money will have interest attached to it at that time. This means that you'll end up paying more than $75.00 for your shoes. If you can prove to lenders that you can responsibly manage debt, you will be in a good position.

Step 3: Pay on Time Each Month

The next step is to make sure that you pay on time each and every month. This is pretty self -explanatory. Early on, missing one payment with a secured credit card can really hurt you in the long run.

Step 4: Check Your Credit Score

After six months, check your credit score and seek out a credit report from your lender to make sure that there are no negative aspects on it. If you see something negative, this will give you a better understanding of how you can do better in the future. Obtaining a full credit report will give you information pertaining to how many lines of credit you currently have open, who has requested to see your credit report, and will also include public records such as foreclosures and bankruptcies that are impacting your overall credit. This information can provide great insight into how your credit works and how your activity contributes to your credit score in total.

Step 5: Apply for an Unsecured Credit Card

Lastly, after a year of spending money with the credit card that required a security deposit, you should start thinking about opening an unsecured credit card, meaning that this credit card requires no down payment. You should wait at least a year to do this because you need to give your secured card time to build and establish your credit first. Additionally, it's important to not apply for many unsecured credit cards simultaneously when it's time to implement this step.

Each time you apply for a new credit card, your credit score goes down in a small way. It's silly to lower your credit score just to apply for many cards at once.

Most important when understanding how to establish credit when you have none at the onset is to have patience. It takes many years to establish yourself as a reliable and good borrower, but the benefits of having good credit are worth the patience that's necessary. You will save an extraordinary amount of money by establishing your credit early in life. It's worth the time you have to spend using unsecured credit cards to obtain this larger goal.

Chapter 10: Improving My Credit Score

Yes, we can improve our Credit Scores by taking affirmative action. Treat the improvement in your credit score like a part time job. If you are unable to secure a low interest consolidation loan to pay off high interest debt, then it is costing you money to have a low credit score. There are penalties for missteps with different types of debt. We can repair low scores quickly by taking the right steps to eliminate bad reports for credit card debt and other loans. We will outline these steps in the next 10 chapters.

Credit Crunch
How housing missteps affect your credit score.

	ESTIMATED STARTING SCORE			APROXIMATE TIME TO RETURN TO ORIGINAL SCORE		
	680	**720**	**780**	680	720	780
30 days late on mortgage	600-620	630-650	670-690	9 months	2.5 years	3 years
Short sale or deed in lieu of foreclosure	610-630	605-625	655-675	3 years	7 years	7 years
Foreclosure or short sale with amount of unpaid balance disclosed	575-595	570-590	620-640	3 years	7 years	7 years

Source: FICO

Credit Repair Step 1

Get a copy of your credit report including your credit score; review the details for accuracy and note any errors.

Look for the following potential errors:

Incorrect late payments, collection amounts and balances written off thus bad.

Credit accounts indicated as non-current - you want to see account history as paid as agreed or according to terms

Negative items older than 7 (10 years for bankruptcy cases) years still showing on your credit report

Credit provider closing accounts when it should be indicated as agreed by both you and the creditor provider

Incorrect balances

Incorrect identification information.

Credit Repair Step 2

Use credit card providers who report credit limits for their cards. In the case where you do not use your credit limit on a card, and the card provider does not report any limit, then the credit agencies can very well estimate a balance higher than the actual amount outstanding.

According to a Nilson's report, approximately $860 billion dollars of consumer debt is outstanding and 98% is in the form of credit card debt.

A few cards which you may want to check out include the following:

American Express 5% cash back

Capital One Aspire

TD Visa

MBNA Mastercard

Go to website **http://www.ratesupermarket.ca/credit_c ards/** to learn more about these cards.

Credit Repair Step 3

If your debt reduction plan indicates that you should close one or more of your credit card accounts, then keep the one(s) which reflect a positive track record of your creditworthiness. The older the retained card the better.

Credit Repair Step 4

Pay off debts which are with the collection agencies and negotiate the removal of this debt history from your credit card report in exchange for payment in full. This option will greatly assist in speeding up the repair of your credit rating.

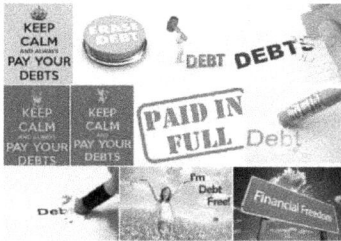

First, you will need to complete a debt reduction plan which is linked to your available funds, etc. I discuss ways to increase your available cash to pay down on debt as well as how to best allocate those funds to your outstanding debt in my debt reduction book.

Credit Repair Step 5

Negotiate the removal of old unpaid bills which are difficult to verify and which you believe are not legitimate. It could be an old retail store bill, utility bill or medical bill. Contact the vendor and convince them to write off the bill or at least agree to settle the bill for a reduced amount on the condition that it is removed from your credit report. This will speed up the repair process for your credit rating.

Get this agreement in writing before you make your settlement payment.

Credit Repair Step 6

Defaulting on student loans is a bad start for students starting out in their adult lives and needing credit to purchase homes and cars, etc. Use available funds to bring your student loan payments up to date.

It will take time to get your loan accounts in good standing. 12 consecutive payments on time can return your Sallie Mae backed student loans in good standing.

You can always negotiate the repair of your student loan rating by bringing your payments up to date and discussing the matter with the student loan provider disclosing any reasonable factors for late payment and requesting that the negative information be erased from your report.

Credit Repair Step 7

Negotiate with your Creditor to remove any negative information on your credit report. Prove to them that you are a good customer and will continue to be and that you will bring any outstanding balances up to date. Business owners want happy customers who will provide positive testimonials about their products and services and want you to continue to be a happy customer.

Credit Repair Step 8

Someone else's account can show up on your credit report if you are an authorized user on their card. Your credit score will benefit from all the positive information on that account and the non-utilized credit. The longer the credit history on the associated account the more boost to your credit score.

Also, the lower the utilization of the associated account the better as it will lower your percentage of used credit to non-utilized credit.

It is well worthwhile for you to convince family members and friends to add you to their accounts; this will fast track the repair to your credit score. You do not need access to any card or information about their account. In fact, add as many good associated accounts as possible.

Credit Repair Step 9

Try to use a maximum of 25% of your credit limit. In other words, pay down any used credit card limit to the 25% threshold with the interest free interval. Revolving loans carry a higher impact on your credit thus warrant your attention first, over installment payment type credit.

87

Consider accepting new credit card offers with a credit limit which will increase your overall limit thus lowering your current utilization percentage. You still need to consider the cost of carrying any credit card in terms of interest rates and annual card dues.

Credit Repair Step 10

Develop a good working relationship with your local bank manager. They are human beings too, and are eager to help their customers who are sincerely trying to improve their personal lives and credit situation. A good bank manager can offer suggestions on financial planning and debt consolidation loans, etc.

Your banker can assist you in preparing a financial plan which will greatly assist in reducing debt and developing a good credit score.

Chapter 11: Understanding The Laws

Many mistakes can be made due to not understanding the laws of the Fair Credit Reporting Act (FCRA) and your states laws on credit reporting.

FCRA was enacted on October 26, 1970 to allow consumers to improve the accuracy of credit reports through the opportunity to challenge and correct negative items. This is a very valuable tool. There is so much information that could be delivered on this topic but, unfortunately, I will only be able to highlight a few. If you would like to review a complete copy of the Fair Credit Reporting Act go to: http://www.ftc.gov/os/statutes/fcradoc.pdf

Also, laws vary from state to state so it is important to research specifics of your state before submitting any disputes to the bureaus. For most states, this information is available from your state's Secretary of State website.

For quick fixes to your credit report, here are a few things for you to consider -

*Statue of Limitations- This is one of the easiest ways to get old collections removed from your credit report. According to the FCRA if a debt is not collected within 7 years from its original delinquent date, then it is to be removed from the report. Most states have a statue of limitations that is generally less then the Federal statue. My state has a 3-year statue of limitations. It is important to understand that Federal law will supercede State law, however, often credit bureaus will remove the disputed collection when a letter stating the statue of limitation of the state is received.

*Duplications - This is a great example of how to clean up the collection section of your credit report rather quickly. FCRA was put in place to ensure that the information reported to the Bureaus is accurate. Frequently, people that have several collections on their report will notice duplicate collections. This happens when a creditor is trying to collect and is unable to do so. They then sell the debt to a collection company for pennies on the dollar. At this point, it is re-reported to the Bureaus as a new collection. It is not unheard of for a collection to be sold 5-6 times. This is an accuracy issue. The problem occurs because the previous collector does report the debt as a Zero balance. Since the previous collector no longer holds that collection, that debt is no longer valid. It is quite simple ... If you no longer owe a debt to a company which appears on your credit report, then that company is not allowed to show you as owing a balance and you can dispute the debt.

*Licensing - This is yet another one of my favorite tricks. This action will require a little bit of research on your part but should still be one of the first things you look at when trying to get a debt removed. Not all companies have valid business license. Sounds Crazy, but its true!! Under your state's Secretary of State Website, you should be able to search records of business entities since this is public information. If that company is not licensed in your state, or their license has expired, then there is a good chance you can get that collection deleted from your report.

*Debt Validation – this is where a company, which holds a debt, has to prove to you that it is actually your debt. Fortunately, for you and I as consumers, this can prove to be rather difficult for the company because their bookkeeping/accounting skills may not be totally accurate. Also, if a debt has changed hands multiple times, the odds are greater that they will be unable to provide you with specific information. If they cannot prove it...then they will have to remove it!!

If they are able to prove it, then it is important that you try to find any inconsistencies and then send in a dispute for having inaccurate information on your report. I have seen cases where debt validation was our last resort and, when we received the information from the collection company, we found that the original date of the collection was over 7 years ago. Little did they realize they actually provided the information needed to get the collection removed due to the statue of limitations.

Chapter 12: How Do I Start My Credit?

Getting credit for the first time, or building up limited credit, may seem hard to do. Most lenders will not want to take the risk.

If you are a college student it is a little easier to get credit. There are many lenders that specialize in lending to college students. Actually credit may come too easy and with few people warning you about the risks of too much credit. Some of these lenders don't care if you can pay the bills now, they are counting on the fact that you will have income later in life and they are willing to wait for you to get your career going. Of course, by then they will have put your account into collection thereby ruining your credit and increasing their fees tremendously. If you get credit, while in school, make sure that you do not borrow more than you can pay. Your credit will determine if you get the job, get the apartment, and get the car loan. Your credit profile is the most valuable thing you own; don't destroy it because you just could not do without that bigger TV or trip to Vegas. Think long term and your life will be better for it.

If you are not a student and are looking to start or increase your credit profile, there are things you can do. First of all, you will need to have income in order to get credit. I know this sounds like it should go without saying, but you would be surprised how many people don't consider this.

One way of establishing credit is to get a secured credit card or loan. This type of account requires that you open a savings account, with the lender, and deposit the same amount of money you wish them to lend you. This savings account will be restricted; you cannot take out the money, and it will be used to guarantee payment on the loan or credit card. The lender is basically lending you your own money and charging you a fee for dealing with the accounting and reporting to the credit bureaus. Since the lender is not risking any money, they will be more willing to give you credit. Not all banks offer this service and you may want to check with credit unions in your area or look for some online. Make sure you confirm with the lender that they do report to all three credit bureaus. You want to work with lenders that report to all three so that you are building your credit profile with all of them. If they only report to one or two bureaus then don't open that account and look for another lender. After 6 months of making payments on time, ask them if they would convert your account to an unsecured account. If they do then you can close the savings account and use that money to open another secured account with a different lender.

Another way of starting credit is to apply for store credit cards with the lower priced stores. Most of these stores will take a chance on you for a small amount of money, usually starting you off with $ 200 to $ 500 in credit. Stores such as Target™, Walmart™, furniture stores, and stores that market to the Spanish community are good places to start. This may mean that you are purchasing something that you really don't need but building credit will cost you some money. Just don't buy anything too expensive. When I was first establishing my credit I went and purchased a slightly overpriced watch ($200) at one of these stores on an installment loan basis. I paid $ 20 a month for the next two years. It helped me get started and it will help you also.

You want to get a total of 2 to 4 credit cards and one installment loan if you can afford it. Just make sure that you can make the payments. Having a bad credit history is worse than not having credit at all. Also remember to use a small portion of the credit card limit, and then pay it off, a couple times a year. For the first year, have a balance owing every month, on the secured credit cards. The lender will not switch the account, to unsecured, until you have a history of making your payments on time.

No balance due = no payment due = no payment history with the lender

No balance may look great on your credit report, but your lender knows the whole story.

Can't find any secured credit cards or more info ? Go to

www.fix-my-score.com

Chapter 13: Credit Action, Scams And Problems

ACTIONS: Are you aware of how many ways there are for thieves to get access to your credit card accounts and make unauthorized charges against them? Simply by rummaging through old receipts that you have thrown out or left somewhere public, or by a shop assistant quickly scribbling down your card details while out of your sight, or by an untrustworthy seller who you deal with on the phone, by mail or the Internet, your private account details can be taken and abused by almost anyone.

While most of these situations are rare, and there are safety measures in place to avoid the abuses they highlight, it is a fact that credit card fraud and identity theft is such an immense, growing problem that it is costing the financial services industry billions of dollars each year. Therefore it is important to be aware of the potential dangers and be familiar with a few simple steps you can take to reduce the risk that you will become the victim of fraud and/or identity theft.

Simple steps that you can take include:

· Sign all of your cards on the signature line on the back as soon as you receive them.

· Consider carrying your cards separately from your wallet and driver's license and insurance cards because the combination of these items exposes a vast amount of information about your private life, such as your name, address, age, history, social security number, etc.

· Always keep your PIN numbers safe and separate from your cards. The best option is to memorize all the numbers and destroy all written copies except a copy safely stored away at home or in a safe deposit box.

· If you card is out of sight during a transaction, try to observe what's going on behind the counter, and seek to get your card back as soon as possible.

· Destroy receipts if you do not need them. If you do need to keep receipts, make sure they are stored away safely at home.

· Carefully check all your monthly statements for your credit cards. If there are any questions, contact your card issuer immediately to resolve the problem.

· Never leave credit cards lying around where others can gain access to them.

· Don't lend your cards to others.

· Don't sign blank receipts.

· Never give your card information over the phone to someone who calls you. If you purchase something by charging on the phone, make sure you initiate the call to the company, so you know who you are talking with.

· If you suspect a fraud or lose your cards, report it immediately to the card issuers so they can put an instant stop on all charges.

SCAMS: Whether you are a first time credit card user or have had credit for years, it is important to know about possible scams that can threaten you. Although most credit card companies are honest, there are also some dishonest ones that want to rip you off. If you are unaware of the ways in which you can be conned or misled, then you could end up losing a lot of money. The following sections identify some of worst credit card scams and how to avoid them.

Debt Suspension

Debt suspension is sometimes offered by banks as part of a credit card contract as a way to "help" you keep on track with card payments if you become unemployed. The way debt suspension works is that you pay a certain amount each month (a fee) so that if you cannot pay your bills then no interest will accrue during this time. Although this might seem like a good idea at first, the benefits are really very minimal. You cannot use your card while you are out of work, and although no interest is being added, your payments are also not being paid. Once you can work again you still have the full balance to pay.

In essence you are paying money for something that will not really help you. If you are getting a new credit card, make sure that this type of debt suspension offer in not included in your contract with a special fee attached. If it is, then get it removed or find another credit card provider. You can also find an independent insurance provider that will help with your payments if you are unemployed.

Advanced Fees

One of the worst scams around is the advanced fees bamboozle, which targets people who are desperate to get a credit card with good rates. In this case the "lender" will offer you a card at a great interest rate, but the catch is you have to pay an advance administrative fee up front before you application can be processed. Once you have paid this fee (which can be several hundred dollars) you probably will never hear from the company again. If you are ever offered a card but are asked to pay a fee upfront, just refuse. Even if you have poor credit you should not have to pay fees upfront for cards. A lender should either accept or reject your application, and fees are not required.

Credit Protection

One of the most common scams is to add expensive credit protection to your card in case it is lost or stolen. The extra money you pay for this protection is usually very high and often covers you for very little. If you report your card stolen immediately, then it is unlikely that you will lose much, and other insurance policies and consumer laws often cover you already. If you really want protection then obtain a policy from an independent company. The expense will be lower, and it will protect all of your cards at once.

Your best scam protection

If you are getting a new credit card, the best thing you can do is to check and double check all clauses within the agreement before you sign it. Many credit card agreements are very detailed and very lengthy, with many pages of fine print. The point about fine print that is buried deep in a written contract is that it is probably information that the lender wants you to "gloss over" instead of carefully reading and understanding. For your financial security, if there is a great deal to read in the contract, tell the lender you will take the document home and study it, then return the next day for a formal signing. If the lender says you can't take the unsigned document home, that is your clue to say goodbye!

If anything in the credit card agreement seems suspicious at all, do not sign it but go and find a different lender. As long as you are aware of the dangers, you will find a fair and honest credit card company that can give you great rates.

Be aware that there are literally hundreds of credit card issuers, and every one of them would like to get you using their card so you can have the privilege of paying them interest and fees month after month. In addition to the dedicated credit card companies (such as Master card, VISA and American Express) many banks, credit unions, other financial institutions and major retail stores issue their own cards, There are cards for personal use, business use, low interest, zero interest, bad credit, excellent credit, prepaid, secured, student cards, reward cards, gas station cards, etc., etc. Most card issuers are honest, but the interest and fee you will pay are largely dependent on the status of your credit score.

PROBLEMS: Retail businesses always cash in on holiday seasons to maximize their sales and profits. It will be high season for them, and they will stock up, price up, and smile all the way to the bank. They know that consumers are less restrained in their spending during holidays than at any other time. Many of those holiday sale prices are merely reductions of greatly jacked-up prices to begin with and are supported by high intensity marketing and advertising efforts. These are the times during the year that encompass the highest credit card activity and additional consumer debt.

Perhaps you are among the many who have suffered post-holiday season financial stress, and you want to make sure it does not happen again. Your success in this will be determined by how well you control three critical factors: (1) your increased rate of spending; (2) the manner in which you finance that spending; and (3) the financial demands that follow in the subsequent months.

A problem many can relate to is financing with plastic. With holidays, such as Christmas, New Year, Valentine's Day, etc. coming around quickly, many people find they have not saved enough for their celebrations. Moreover, budgeting is an alien concept during this time and spending can spiral out of control. To cover the inevitable shortfall in resources, the credit card is an obvious attraction. There are advantages to using the card to finance your expenditures:

· It gives you free access to a month's worth of credit

· It gives you the temporary ability to spend beyond your means

· It allows you to track you expenditures with your monthly statement

· You do not have to carry lots of cash around with you

Us of the credit card, however, does carry with it significant dangers if it is not carefully controlled. It is very easy to vastly increase you spending (by more than 50%) when using a credit card compared with using cash. The following are some key principles to help you guard against running into credit card debt trouble.

Make a spending plan

If your spending is going to exceed your income during the festive months, consider cutting intended festive expenses, or other expenses, to stay within your income. If you don't have one, draw up a spending plan for the period of time in question. Don't be shortsighted and think your credit card will come to the rescue. Though not readily apparent, the use of your credit card can easily create distortions in the management of your finances. Unless you are monitoring both your cash and credit spending, there is a danger of living way beyond your means. It would therefore be unwise to begin using a credit card if you are not in control of your finances that are reflected in your spending plan.

Track your debt-to-income ratio

You must keep in mind that use of your credit card immediately adds to your indebtedness. In managing your financial affairs, a key indicator to watch is your debt/income ratio. This is the monthly debt repayment as a percentage of your monthly after-tax income. It should raise a red flag when you tinker with too much debt. As a general rule, a ratio that rises over 20% is becoming unhealthy. If you already have credit card debt that is overdue or over the limit, do not add to it.

Using credit card as a finance bridge

Use of a credit card is ideally a means of short-term financing of your operations. That means settling any debt incurred with your card should be paid off within the first payment period, resulting in no finance charges. Paying the minimum balance will not do. If you are not confident that you can pay it off in full, you do yourself a huge favor by not using the credit card. Should you decide to go ahead and use the card, you need to be prepared for extra costs in interest and penalties associated with extended credit. This adds to your expenses, and you need to be ready to reduce other regular expense to accommodate this; otherwise you run the risk of creating ongoing hard-core debt.

Track your net worth

In simplest terms your net worth is the value of all of your assets (everything you own outright) minus the value all of your liabilities (everything you owe). Credit card debt is a liability. Credit card debt that people incur during the festive season is typically for consumer spending, such as holiday gifts, entertainment and travel, and this is known as consumer debt. This kind of debt adds to your liabilities, but contributes nothing to your assets. Thus your net worth is reduced to the extent of consumer debt incurred. Shrinking net worth on a continuing basis is not good for your financial health. So you should plan on having a happy holiday season, but as you go about it, maintain your finances so that you won't be debt-laden after the next credit card payment cycle.

Consumer spending is different from a fixed installment payment, such as a mortgage. A mortgage payment (which is a liability) is somewhat offset by an asset (increased equity in your house). Typically homeownership will increase your net worth because of increasing equity and increasing value of your house over the life of the mortgage.

Chapter 14: Avoid Common Credit Score

Mistakes

There are a few things that people do without realizing it that have a bad effect on their credit score. Follow these tips to avoid the common traps that can sink your credit risk rating:

Tip #11: Beware of debts and credit you don't use. It is easy today to apply for a store credit card that you forget all about in three years - but that account will remain on your credit report and affect your credit score as long as it is open. Having credit lines and credit cards you don't need makes you seem like a worse credit risk because you run the risk of "overextending" your credit.

Also, having lots of accounts you don't use increases the odds that you will forget about an old account and stop making payments on it - resulting in a lowered credit score. Keep only your used accounts and make sure that all other accounts are closed. Having fewer accounts will make it easier for you to keep track of your debts and will increase the chances of you having a good credit score.

However, realize that when you close an account, the record of the closed account remains on your credit report and can affect your credit score for a while. In fact, closing unused credit accounts may actually cause your credit score to drop in the short term, as you will have higher credit balances spread out over a smaller overall credit account base.

For example, if your unused accounts amounted to $2000 and you owe $1000 on accounts that you have now (let's say on two credit cards that total $2000) you have gone from using one fourth of your credit ($1000 owed on a possible $4000 you could have borrowed) to using one half of your credit (you owe $1000 from a possible $2000). This will actually cause your credit risk rating to drop. In the long term, though, not having extra temptation to charge and not having credit you don't need can work for you.

Tip #12: Be careful of inquiries on your credit report. Every time that someone looks at your credit report, the inquiry is noted. If you have lots of inquiries on your report, it may appear that you are shopping for several loans at once - or that you have been rejected by lenders. Both make you appear a poor credit risk and may affect your credit score. This means that you should be careful about who looks at your credit report. If you are shopping for a loan, shop around within a short period of time, since inquiries made within a few days of each other will generally be lumped together and counted as one inquiry.

You can also cut down on the number of inquiries on your account by approaching lenders you have already researched and may be interest in doing business with - by researching first and approaching second you will likely have only a few lenders accessing your credit report at the same time, which can help save your credit score.

Tip #13: Be careful of online loan rate comparisons. Online loan rate quotes are easy to get - type in some personal information and you can get a quote on your car loan, personal loan, student loan, or mortgage in seconds. This is free and convenient, leading many people to compare several companies at once in order to make sure that they get the best deal possible.

The problem is that since online quotes are a fairly recent phenomenon, credit bureaus count each such quote estimate as an "inquiry." This means that if you compare too many companies online by asking for quotes, your credit score will fall due to too many "inquiries."

This does not mean that you shouldn't seek online quotes for loans - not at all. In fact, online loan quotes are a great resource that can help you get the very best rates on your next loan. What this information does mean, however, is that you should research companies and narrow down possible lenders to just a few before making inquiries. This will help ensure that the number of inquires on your credit report is small - and your credit rating will stay in good shape.

Tip #14: Don't make the mistake of thinking that you only have one credit report. Most people speak of having a "credit score" when in fact most people have at least three or more scores - and these scores can vary widely. There are three major credit bureaus in the country that develop credit reports and calculate credit scores. There are also a number of smaller credit bureau companies.

Plus, some larger lenders calculate their own credit risk scores based on information in your credit report. When repairing your credit score, then, you should not focus on one number - at the very least, you need to contact the three major credit bureaus and work on repairing the three credit scores separately. Tip #15: Don't make the mistake of closing lots of credit accounts just to improve your score. This seems like a contradiction, but it really is not. Many people think that to improve their credit score, they just have to pay off some debts and close their accounts. This is not exactly accurate. There are several reasons to think carefully before closing your accounts.

First, if you close an account you need (for example, if you close all your credit card accounts) then you will have to reapply for credit, and all those inquiries from lenders will cause your credit score to actually drop.

Secondly, most credit bureaus give high favorable points to those who have a good long-term credit history. That means that closing the credit card account you have had since college may actually hurt you in the long run. If you have credit accounts that you don't use or if you have too many credit lines, then by all means pay off some and close them. Doing so may help your credit score - but only if you don't close long-term accounts you need. In general, close the most recent accounts first and only when you are sure you will not need that credit in the near future. Closing your accounts is a bad idea if:

1) You will be applying for a loan soon. The closing of your accounts will make your credit score drop in the short term and will not allow you to qualify for good loan rates.

2) Closing your accounts will make your overall debt balance too high. If you owe $10 000 now and closing some accounts would leave you with only $1000 of possible credit, you are close to maxing out your credit - which gives you a bad credit rating.

In the short term, closing accounts will lower your credit score, but in the long run it can be beneficial.

Tip #16: Don't assume that one thing will boost your credit score a specific number of points. Some debtors are lead to believe that paying off a credit card bill will boost their credit score by 50 points while closing an unused credit account will result in 20 more points. Credit scores are certainly not this clear-cut or simple.

How much any one action will affect your credit score is impossible to gauge. It will depend on several factors, including your current credit score and the credit bureau calculating your credit score.

In general, though, the higher your credit score, the more small factors - such as one unpaid bill can affect you. However, when repairing your credit score, you should not be equating specific credit repair tasks with numbers. The idea is to do as many things as you can to get your credit score as close to 800 as you are able. Even if you can improve your credit score by 100 points or so, you will qualify for better interest rates.

Tip #17: Don't think that having no loans or debts will improve your credit score. Some people believe that owing no money, having no credit cards, and in fact avoiding the whole world of credit will help improve their credit score. The opposite is true - lenders want to see that you can handle credit, and the only way they can tell is if you have credit that you handle responsibly. Having no credit at all can actually be worse for your credit score than having a few credit accounts that you pay off scrupulously. If you currently have no credit accounts at all, opening a low balance credit card can actually boost your credit score.

Tip #18: Never do anything illegal to help boost your credit score. It seems pretty obvious, but plenty of people try to lie about their credit scores or even falsify their loan applications because they are ashamed of a bad score. Not only is this illegal, but it is also completely ineffective. Your credit score is easy to check and not only will you not fool lenders by lying but you may actually find yourself facing legal action as a result of your dishonesty.

Chapter 15: How To Check Your Credit

Report For Errors?

Credit reports as powerful as they may be are unfortunately not foolproof. Credit reports can suffer from errors which will hurt your credit reputation. However financially responsible you are, your discipline may not be properly reflected on your credit report. This is why it is important to be vigilant on your credit report.

Statistics show that anywhere from 1 to 4 out every 5 credit reports have errors. Out of those statistics, 5% were denied applications because of erroneous reporting. 10% of those who discovered the errors were able to adjust their scores by more than 50 points. While the credit agencies are responsible for generating the report, you are responsible for the accuracy of the report itself.

A telltale sign that there is an error in your report is by comparing all three reports for the agencies. If your credit score is noticeably different or has a large discrepancy from one report to another, then this means that one, two or all three are missing data which the other agency has.

There are generally three sources of errors in your credit report:

1.Data sources

2.   Time lapses

3.   Fraud

4.   Time delays

5.   Persona information

Most errors do not come from the credit agency itself but the sources of their data. For example, your bank may have overlooked sending an updated status of your credit card account. Even though you have paid the amount in full, in your credit report, an outstanding balance still exists.

Another error is one time lapses. Take note that any history of bad debts, whether paid or unpaid, will appear within 7 years. Bankruptcy will be listed in your report for 10 years. Make sure that you count the years since you have failed to pay the debt. If your bad debt is still listed after 7 years, then that is a credit report error.

Identity theft is rampant with the various modus operandi for stealing credit card information. If you fail to notice unauthorized transactions on your bank statement, then any unpaid transactions will still be included in your credit report.

Also each of the credit agencies has their own cut off periods in generating their report. It may not be a matter of erroneous reporting but only of delayed reporting. One agency may have generated a report on your most recent payment while the other agency will report on the next period.

There will also be errors if you have been using different names, such as aliases, in your financial transactions. This will result to a credit report that is fragmented, with one set of data found on your real name and the other on another name. Other discrepancies may also be a result of varying personal information such as inaccuracies in social security numbers, addresses or a change of last name for newly married women.

Any dispute you make must be well-documented. For example, if you have fully paid a loan but the report says you still have an outstanding balance, you need to provide a copy of the receipt of full payment. Any communication you make with your bank or financial institution must be put in writing and then the credit agency must be furnished a copy of your letter.

If you are sending by postal service or by email, request a return receipt or a notification that the letter has been received. Include the confirmation of receipt in your documents for dispute. Usually, the credit agency is given 30 days to investigate and verify your dispute. In turn, the creditor is given another 30 days to either confirm or reject your dispute.

If the creditor does not respond within 30 days of the agency's notification, then the entry must be deleted. If there is any delay in your dispute, you may ask the credit agency to include your statement of dispute on your credit report. Although it is your responsibility to verify your credit report, it is the credit agency that is responsible for correcting it.

When you write a dispute, it is best to provide all information. Identify exactly the specifics of your dispute, the item, the amount, the status or any detail that is erroneous. Next, state the facts and your position on the dispute. Finally, you need to request for changes in the credit report either by correcting or deleting the figures. Write professionally and avoid any negative, threatening or emotionally laden remarks.

Here is a sample of a dispute letter:

[Your Name]
[Your Address]
[Your City, State, Zip Code]
[Date]

Complaint Department
[Company Name]
[Street Address]
[City, State, Zip Code]

Dear Sir or Madam:

I am writing to dispute the following information in my file. I have circled the items I dispute on the attached copy of the report I received.

This item [identify item(s) disputed by name of source, such as creditors or tax court, and identify type of item, such as credit account, judgment, etc.] is [inaccurate or incomplete] because[describe what is inaccurate or incomplete and why]. I am requesting that the item be removed [or request another specific change] to correct the information.

Enclosed are copies of [use this sentence if applicable and describe any enclosed documentation, such as payment records and court documents] supporting my position. Please reinvestigate this[these] matter[s] and [delete or correct] the disputed item[s] as soon as possible.

Sincerely,

Your name

Enclosures: [List what you are enclosing.]

This letter can be found at: http://www.consumer.ftc.gov/articles/0384-sample-letter-disputing-errors-your-credit-report

When you have an accurate credit report that is reflective of your true credit standing, then you can enjoy the benefits of your financial discipline.

Your credit report is your credit reputation. The better it is, the easier your financial life will be. For example, you can get approval of your loan faster just by your score. While before it took banks or financial institutions weeds or even months to evaluate your loan application, today with credit scores they have an instant measurement for your capacity to pay and financial discipline.

Also the credit report makes processing of your loans fairer, it can remove bias based on gender, race, religion, marital status and other personal information. Most lenders have the tendency to evaluate you beyond your financial capacity. With a credit report, they can focus only on what is essential in qualifying you for a loan. Past credit history may be corrected as you improve your financial responsibility. This was once impossible when a bad debt becomes a permanent fixture in your records.

More loans are also made possible because lenders can offer you a wide range of products that matches your score. Instead of a few standard products that may disqualify you in your application, lenders can adjust their offer based on your score, instead of denying you altogether. With credit reports, lenders are able to reduce the cost of their credit investigation activities. In turn, they are able to offer lower interest rates. For example, the United States enjoys lower interest rates compared to European countries because of the availability of credit reports.

Chapter 16: How To Stop The Pain & The Emotional Drain

In this chapter, you will become educated on specific laws that stop the individual as well as companies from treating you any way they feel. The passages below will empower you with the knowledge that will cause you to tell a Collection Company, "You are not allowed to do this, and you must stop."

After a validation of debt has occurred it is time for you to acknowledge what you actually owe.

The most stressful position to be in is to have faced a financial hardship such as a death of a breadwinner or a personal job loss. To make matters worse, you then have to turn around and deal with a debt collector harassing you throughout the day. It is mentally painful to have a company calling you over and over asking you to fulfill an obligation in which you may not be in the position to pay.

Additionally, it is also emotionally draining when that debt is also entwined with past experiences that bring up negative emotions. The last and most dangerous effects of dealing with Collection Companies is that it makes most people feel trapped in a corner. This fact, in turn, forces you to make bad financial decisions.

As the saying goes, "Desperate times calls for desperate measures." You know this is true if you ever felt so trapped that you had to turn to a payday loan store that charges such unbelievably high-interest rates, it is not even funny. Even worst, if you turned to a Credit Repair Company out of desperation to fix your credit problems, you can end up paying a whopping $99.00 per month. This statement means you now have allowed your past pain to cause a greater financial drain. The first way to stop the pain is to know what a debt collector is allowed and not allowed to do to you in accordance with the law.

The Fair Debt Collection Practices Act was established to protect American consumers against abusive practices by Collection Companies and individuals.

The Fair Debt Collection Practices Act was instituted for you to stop the painful process of dealing with blatantly abusive collection tactics. The surprising part of the Fair Debt Collection Act is that the lawmakers actually admit that the offensive tactics of the debt collectors contributed to several painful results. The top negative consequences were personal bankruptcies, marital instability, the loss of jobs, and the invasion of individual privacy.

In order to prohibit the above from reoccurring, lawmakers have added the following parameters. The below regulations have been categorized in who, what, when, where, how, and why format in order to simplify it for your overall benefit and to maximize its use and application:

*To whom can debt collectors communicate?

Debt Collectors CAN:

-communicate with any person other than the consumer for the purpose of getting information on the location of the consumer only after they identify themselves while stating that they are confirming or correcting the location of the consumer.

Debt Collectors CAN NOT:

-communicate with anyone other than the consumer more than once unless requested by such persons or unless the debt collector thinks that the earlier response from such persons is erroneous or incomplete.

*When can debt collectors communicate?

Debt Collectors CAN NOT:

-call a client after 8:00pm or before 9:00am, local time at the consumer's location, except with prior consent of the consumer given directly to the debt collector or the express permission of a court of competent jurisdiction.

*Where can debt collectors communicate?

Debt Collectors CAN NOT:

-call the consumer's place of employment if the debt collector knows or has reason that the consumer's employer prohibits the consumer from receiving such communication, except with prior consent of the consumer given directly to the debt collector or the express permission of a court of competent jurisdiction.

*How can debt collectors communicate?

Debt Collectors CAN NOT:

-send communication by postcard

-send communication revealing that the item mailed or telegrammed is from the debt collector or is related to a debt.

*Why
can debt collectors continue to communicate with you?

Debt Collectors CAN NOT:

-communicate further with the consumer with respect to such debt, if a consumer notifies a debt collector in writing that the consumer refuses to pay a debt or that the consumer wishes the debt collector to cease further communication with them.

Debt Collectors CAN:

-communicate with the consumer even after a written request to cease communication, as an exception, in order to advise the consumer that the debt collector's further efforts are being terminated.

-communicate with the consumer even after a written request to cease communication, as an exception, in order to notify that the debt collector or creditor may invoke specified remedies which are ordinarily invoked by such debt collector or creditor.

*What can debt collectors communicate?

Debt Collectors CAN NOT:

-state that the consumer they are trying to locate owes any debt when communicating to anyone outside the consumer responsible for the debt.

-use or threat of use of violence or other criminal means to harm the physical person, reputation, or property of any such person

-use obscene or profane language that is to abuse the hearer or reader.

-create a publication of a list of consumers who allegedly refused to pay debts, except to a consumer reporting agency as an example.

-advertise the sale of any debt to coerce payment of the debt

-cause a telephone to ring or engaging any person in a telephone conversation repeatedly or continuously with intent to annoy, abuse, or harass any person at the called number.

-use any false, deceptive, or misleading representation or means in connection with the collection of any debt.

-use false representation or implication that nonpayment of any debt will result in arrest or imprisonment of any person or the seizure, garnishment, attachment, or sale of any property or wages of any person unless such action is lawful and the debt collector or creditor intends to take such action.

-use false representation or implication that the consumer committed any crime or other conduct in order to disgrace the consumer.

-communicate or threatening to communicate to any person credit information that is known or which should be known to be false, including the failure to communicate that a disputed debt is disputed.

-accept from any person a check or other payment instrument postdated by more than 5 days, the only exception is if the consumer is notified in writing of the debt collector's intent to deposit the actual check or other payment instrument between 3 business days to (maximum) 10 business days before the actual deposit.

For example, the exception states if a check is postdated 30 day out or let's specifically use postdated for the 30th of January – you as the consumer must receive notification in writing of the debt collector's intent to deposit the actual check between January 27th (3 business days out) and January 16th (Maximum 10 business days out) before the actual postdated deposit occurs on January 30th.

-solicit or ask for any postdated check or other postdated payment instrument for the purpose of threatening or instituting criminal prosecution.

-deposit or threaten to deposit any postdated check or other posted payment instrument prior to the date on such check or instrument.

In case, you are encountering one of the above, I first want to provide you with two of the most effective letters in halting all forms of harassment and abuse directed towards you.

Letter #1: "Requesting To Cease All Forms of Communication With Me" [Click Here to obtain your free copy of this letter that a request that all forms of collection calls and mail stop]

Letter #2: "Requesting To Only Contact My Lawyer And To Cease All Forms of Communication With Me"

[Click Here to obtain your free copy of this letter for those who have attained a lawyer. This letter is requesting that all future forms of communication go directly to your lawyer and to cease any further forms of communication with you]

In addition to the above letters, if you have experienced or are currently experiencing one of the above abusive collection practices then this next section is for you. I will teach you step-by- step on how to file a complaint and how to finally stop the emotional rollercoaster.

Similarly to the first book, it is recommended to get CFPB, Consumer Financial Protection Bureau, involved to back your efforts in filling a complaint.

Its best practice to file a complaint with the CFPB, Consumer Financial Protection Bureau, because their job is to make sure all consumers are safe from abuse, deceptive and unfair practices.

Investopedia defines CFPB – CONSUMER FINANCIAL PROTECTION BUREAU:

As a regulatory agency charged with overseeing financial products and services that are offered to consumers. The Consumer Financial Protection Bureau is divided into several units, including research, community affairs, consumer complaints, the Office of Fair Lending and the Office of Financial Opportunity. These units work together to protect and educate consumers about the various types of financial products and services that are available.

Below are the counseled steps that should be read carefully and followed in its entirety:

Step #1 - Go to the CFPB Website: www.consumerfinance.gov

Step #2 – Click on the "Submit a complaint" tab which is the last tab at the top right of the page.

Step #3 – Click on "Submit a complaint."

Step #4 – Once directed to the "Submit a complaint" page under the "Products and Services" category click on "Debt Collection"

Step #5 – The next screen will state: "Submit a credit reporting complaint to the CFPB," click the "Get started" button which will take you to...

Step #6 – Section #1: What happened?

Under the question: "What type of debt is this?" Click on the individual debt that you are addressing. The following options are:

*Credit card

*Medical

*Auto

*Federal Student Loan

*Non-federal Student Loan

*Mortgage

*Payday Loan

*Other (i.e. phone, health club, etc.)

*I do not know

Step #7 – The next question is, "Which of these best describes your issues?" Below are the categories and the additional drop-down options to choose from in their respective category:

Communication Tactics:

Frequent or repeated calls

Called outside of 8am to 9pm

Used Obscene,
profane or other abusive language

Threatened to take legal action

Called after sent written cease of communication notice

Continued attempts to collect debt I do not owe:

Debt was discharged in bankruptcy

Debt resulted from identity theft

Debt was paid

Debt is not mine

Disclosure verification of the debt:

Did not receive notice of right to dispute

Not enough information to verify the debt (i.e. amount of debt & name of the creditor)

Did not disclose the communication was a n attempt to collect a debt

False statements or representation:

Attempted to collect wrong amount (Chec k Matching up)

Impersonated attorney, law enforcement or government official

Indicated committing crime by not paying a debt

Indicated should not respond to a lawsuit

Improper contact or sharing of informatio n:

Contacted me after I asked not to

Contacted my employer

Contacted me instead of my attorney

Talked to a third party about my debt

Taking or threatening to take an illegal acti on:

Threatened to arrest me or take me to jail if I do not pay

Threatened to sue me   on   a debt that is too old to be sued on

144

Sued me without properly notifying me of a lawsuit

Sued me where I did not live or did not sign for a debt

Attempt to/Collected exempt funds (i.e. Unemployment, Child Support, etc.)

Seized or attempted to seize property

Step #8 – The next box labeled, "Describe what happened so we can understand the issue" gives you the opportunity to write out the full story. In your description, it is suggested to explain who, what, when, why, and how the violation of rights occurred. The CFPB allows 3900 characters in order to capture all details.

Step #9 – The last section at the bottom of the page is the "Desired Resolution" section in which they are asking you, "What do you think would be a fair resolution of your issue?" This section gives you the opportunity to explain what you think should happen. For example, if they are guilty of improper contact or sharing of information then within this box you should fully explain how such as, all future contact should have gone to your attorney.

Step #10 - Section #2: Company Information

Fill out as much information about the Collection Company as possible as CFPB uses this information to go after them on your behalf. The last section on this page asks you to upload any supporting documentation which is highly recommended. The supporting documentation gives the evidence and your case much more validity.

Step #11 - Section #3: Consumer Information

Fill out the required personal contact infor mation.

Step #12 - Section #4: Review

Review all of the information that you inputted in the previous four sections and then click the submit button.

Please note: The CFPB discloses the following, "CFPB cannot act as my lawyer, a court of law or a financial advisor." To this end, if further legal action results, I recommend that you find an FCRA Attorney.

As previously recommended, please follow the below steps in order to find an FCRA Attorney in your area.

Below are the counseled steps that should be read carefully and followed in its entirety:

Step #1 - Go to the NACA Website: www.naca.net

Step #2 - Click on "Find an Attorney"

Step #3 - Click the State that you reside in.

Step #4 - Click and input your zip code

Step #5 – Click on the drop box option "100 Miles"

(This option is recommended because the more choices you have the better. Moreover, every attorney on the list might not handle an FCRA case).

Step #6 – Click on the attorney's name that is the closest to you in proximity of your zip code.

Step #7 – Look under "Area of Practice" and then under "Credit Reports" to check and see if they handle **"FCRA"** cases, if not, repeat the above steps until you find the closest attorney that does handle FCRA cases.

Please Note: I recommend that you have supporting documentation and actual evidence of the abusive, deceptive and unfair practices before proceeding with legal action. One thing will always be true when it comes to any court case, "Evidence is Everything."

Lastly, I am providing a quick Fox News Investigation video referencing the truthful harsh reality of deceptive, abusive, and harassing practices of Collection Companies.**[Click here to view]**

Points to remember:

*Abusive, deceptive and unfair practices stop with your comprehension of the laws.

*The surprising part of the Fair Debt Collection Practices Act, is that the lawmakers even admit that the abusive tactics of the debt collectors contributed to several painful results. The top negative consequences were personal bankruptcies, marital instability, the loss of jobs, and the invasion of individual privacy.

In the next chapter, I will show you the strategies and timelines for effective negotiation. I will explain to you how the duration of your debt determines the denomination of your payment...

Chapter 17: When To Increase Your Credit Limit

Of course, even if you know why and how to ask for this, you still have to know the right time, as timing is everything. Here are a couple of tips.

– **Not right before you plan to apply for a large loan** – Often, requesting an increase will result in a hard credit inquiry, which will hurt your credit score in the short term (don't worry, the long-term effect of better credit utilization would more than make up for the short term dip). Thus, if you plan on applying for a mortgage or car loan within the next 6 months to a year, I wouldn't request an increase.

– **Well before you need it** – Again, this goes back to the fact that if you are desperate, the creditor will not increase your limit. If you think there will be a time in the future where you will need that extra credit, the time to request an increase is before that. Obviously, it's tough to predict, but you have to be able to look ahead as best as possible.

A good way to get yourself into big financial trouble is to ask for a credit limit just because you want a little bit of extra money to spend. Do not do this. It goes without saying, but if you just want a higher limit just so you can spend more money (and not pay it off right away), that is always a bad idea, and can really damage your financial future.

WHAT IS MY CREDIT LIMIT?

When it comes to your credit limit, the most basic piece of data to know is what your limit actually is. Before you can decide if you want more, you have to actually know what you currently have. There are a couple easy ways to check:

– **It should be listed on your statement** – When I check my credit card statement (either in a paper copy or online), it gives me a summary of the account. That summary usually includes the total balance, the total amount due, the total amount of my limit, and the amount of my available credit. This should be the same for all credit cards.

– You can give them a call – There should be an 800 number on the back of your card. If you give them a call, they should be able to tell you your limit.

As you can see, it's pretty easy! If you are not sure what your credit limit is, do one of these things and find out!

HOW A CREDIT LIMIT INCREASE IMPACTS CREDIT SCORE

When talking about a **credit limit increase**, many people are concerned that this could have a negative effect on their credit score. Is their concern justified? Yes and no.

Asking for an increase on your credit limit can negatively affect your credit score in the short-term. Because it can cause a hard credit inquiry, that will cause the score to dip. That is why I would not recommend asking for an increase any time near to when you will be applying for a mortgage, car loan, or anything else where your interest rate will be dependent on your credit score.

However, in the long run, the better credit utilization from a higher credit limit will more than make up for that short term dip. Thirty percent of your score is determined by the amounts that you owe, and the percentage of amounts that you owe compared to your limits. Assuming you do not spend in proportion to your increase (a not insignificant point), the higher limit will lower your credit utilization percentage, which will increase your score.

So in summary... asking for an increase to your credit limit could hurt you in the very short term, but help you out in the long term. As we have talked about, it will help your credit utilization which will have a positive impact on your score.

STRENGHTEN YOUR CASE FOR A CREDIT LIMIT INCREASE

If you are asking for an increase to your credit limit, the worst case scenario is that you will be denied. This could cause a dip in your credit score (from the credit inquiry), while not giving you all of the benefits of an increased limit.

So, you obviously want to do as good of a job as you can of making sure that the creditor will grant your request, and increase your limit. How can you do that? Here are some tips to help:

– **Make sure your bills are paid on time** – If you have paid any bills late, it probably isn't a good time to ask for an increase. You need to have a good track record of paying your bills in a timely manner, so the creditor knows that you can be trusted with a higher limit.

– **Pay down the bill on the credit card** – If you are close to your limit on the card, asking for more will make it seem like you are desperate, and companies are not necessarily interested in throwing more money to a desperate person, since that could be risky on their part. Pay down the bill as much as you can, THEN ask for the increase.

– **Pay down any other other debts too, if possible** – You will want to do everything you can to show the creditor that you will be able to pay down the card no matter the limit. With as little other debt as possible, this will make them feel more comfortable.

– **Time is your friend** – If you just opened a card, 2 months later is not the right time to ask. Wait until you have had it for awhile, and have built up some time and trust with the company. That will give you a much better likelihood of success.

If you have taken the step to try and increase your limit, the last thing you want to have happen is to have your request turned down, since that means you probably won't be able to ask again for quite a while. So, take the time before hand and make sure your case is as strong as can be.

Chapter 18: Eliminate Debt

(Knowing When You Have a Debt Problem)

Overall well-being does not only refer to physical, mental and emotional health. Financial wellness contributes to our well-being as well. Unfortunately, some of us overlook, or worse, deliberately ignore our financial health when it comes to debt.

But, there are times when we have to take some time out and take stock of our finances, and not just how much we earn and spend. It is easy ignore the amount of debt we've incurred until we apply for a loan, want to rent a house or even get a job. That's when our credit scores reveal just how much debt we truly have.

One indicator of financial health is one's debt-to-income ratio. Experts recommend that a person owe, at most, 20% of their net take-home pay. For example, a person earning $1000 a month should keep his debt below $200 a month. If his car payment is that amount, he shouldn't think about incurring other debts.

But that is an ideal situation, and the reality is that most of us owe far more than 20% of our monthly pay. We still tend to find ourselves buried up to our eyeballs in debt, and often feel helpless as to how to get out of it.

Common Causes of Debt Problems

Debt problems, or "credit problems" can be caused by several behaviors. The most common causes are listed below:

1.   Overspending, or spending beyond one's financial means

2.   Reckless spending, or incurring unnecessary expenses

3.   Poor budgeting, which can be either the inability to come up with a budget, or failure to adhere to a budget which is already in place

4.   Making bad investments

5.   Unforeseen circumstances, such as emergencies, job loss, health issues, and even death

So how do you know when you have a debt problem? If you've ever found yourself in any of the following situations, you may have debt and credit problems.

·You are often late in paying, or scrambling to meet your payment due dates.

·You tap into your savings to pay bills and even basic necessities such as groceries.

·More than half of your monthly income goes towards paying debts.

·You are no longer able to add to your savings.

·You have no savings, period.

·You use credit cards, or borrow money from other people, to pay for regular items that you used to pay for using cash, such as groceries, medicines, and even meals.

·You are use cash advances from your credit cards to pay off other bills.

·You can pay only the minimum payments on your credit cards.

·You've maxed more than one credit card.

·Your credit card balances increase every month due to continuous purchases, despite you making regular payments.

·You no know exactly how much you owe.

·You constantly argue with family members about money.

·You avoid calls from creditors and collectors.

·You're several months behind on bill payments.

·Your bank account is overdrawn or you've bounced a check or two.

·You have experienced being denied credit.

You may have experienced another example that wasn't listed, but they are all serious and must be remedied.

If you lost your job tomorrow would you be able to get by – paying for your basic necessities AND paying your debts – until you find another job?

If someone in your family suddenly fell ill and you had to shoulder all the medical bills, would you be able to survive financially?

If you are more than sure that you'd face immediate financial crisis if one of the above happened, then it is safe to say that you have a debt problem. It's time to take action to prevent it from turning into a major disaster.

Chapter 19: Start Repairing Your Credit

Right, now we are ready to start working on building a better credit profile for you going forward. Remember that it is the latest data that bears the strongest weight in the calculation of your credit score and so what you start doing from today can have an impact, even if you only start off slowly.

Pay Your Bills on Time

Once the arrears are settled, you need to ensure that you pay each and every single one of your bills when it is due, where possible, even paying early if you can.

Also, take into account the time it will take to process your payment when deciding when to pay your bills. If for example, you pay your bills by mailing a check, you need to ensure that there is enough time for the check to reach the company concerned and to be banked before your bill is due.

This is possibly the best way to demonstrate to potential creditors and existing ones that you are becoming more responsible when it comes to managing your credit and that you are managing your debt in a more responsible manner.

Paying your bills on time has an enormously positive impact on your credit rating. It is important to note that here I am not just referring to paying off credit agreements but also to paying off your other monthly bills like gas, cable, etc. Most companies that have ongoing agreements with their clients will report payment history to at least one of the credit bureaus.

Your aim must be to pay everything on time – paying any bill, no matter how small, late every month sends a strong message to a potential creditor – that you are either over-indebted or that you cannot manage your money. After all, let's say you keep paying a gas bill of $40 a month late – how can you be trusted with a loan or credit card installment that is two or three times the amount if you cannot handle a small bill like that?

Stop Maxing out Your Credit

At the height of my credit craziness, I had 11 credit cards, 7 store cards, 4 personal loans and a mortgage, totaling thousands of dollars. I actually got to a stage where I stopped opening my mail because I was scared to face reality.

Naturally, I tried to apply for another loan in order to help me out – I thought it was my only option – and I was horrified when it was declined due to over-indebtedness. I couldn't understand it – I was paying all my accounts on time and doing everything "right". Except that, I was maxing out my cards every single month. I would make a payment and then immediately draw the money out again, usually on the same day.

As a result, my credit rating dropped faster – if you are using the full credit limit available to you, you are showing the creditors that you are battling to manage the debt. Think about it for a second, someone who is comfortably off will not usually max out all their cards constantly, they do not need to.

Once your arrears have been caught up, and you are paying your bills on time every month, start looking at how you can reduce your balances on your credit accounts. Remember, for you to have an excellent score, you need to aim for a credit usage ratio of no more than 30% of your credit limit.

Start rethinking what you are buying on your accounts or credit cards.

Time Your Withdrawals Carefully

If you have no choice but to use the full credit limit every month, time your withdrawals more carefully. Leave at least two to three days between the time that you pay the card and the time that you withdraw the money so that your card is not constantly maxed out. This will also help you to save a little in terms of credit interest.

Another tip that works quite well is to pay your whole grocery allowance into your card and buy as and when necessary –

while the allowance is still in your card, it is reducing your overall balance and doing you some good at the same time. (Only use the allowance, though, not the credit limit here.)

You can also try changing the date of payments of non-interest bearing accounts. Say, for example, that you get paid on the last day of every month and that your insurance payment goes through on the 1st of every month. Can you move the date to the 15th and store the money in an accessible credit card or your access mortgage bond from the date you got paid until just before the payment is due? If you have the self-discipline to make this work, you can save a lot in terms of interest and can also help to improve your credit score at the same time.

Pay More than the Monthly Minimum

Paying only the monthly minimum on your debt is a sign of a borrower who is either irresponsible or one who is over-indebted and negatively impacts your credit rating.

Look at all your revolving credit facilities and see how you can go about paying extra into each of these monthly. This, in itself, will help to improve your credit rating because it indicates that you can not only afford the debt that you have but that you can pay more than strictly necessary. It also helps to reduce the balance faster.

You would be amazed at how much faster your debt will reduce when you start paying more than the minimum monthly installment. Remember that the interest charged is calculated on the daily balance used so everything you do to reduce that balance is helping you – even if it means paying an extra ten dollars a month.

Pay Down Your Debt

You knew that this one was coming – it is advice that we hear all the time. Nevertheless, it is really good advice. You need to start targeting specific accounts in order to either pay them off or to pay them right down.

As you are paying more than the monthly minimum on all your credit accounts, you can now separate the credit accounts into two basic categories – revolving credit and installment credit.

Remember how we discussed that revolving credit was a more open-ended agreement? It is best to keep only one or two of these accounts at most and to ensure that they are way within their limits. Start by targeting the account with the highest interest rate and pay as much extra money into it as possible on a monthly basis. When it is paid off, apply that payment to the account with the next highest interest rate until that is paid off and so on, until all your accounts are paid off.

Choose one or two credit cards and store cards with the best deals in terms of fees and interest and close all the rest down completely.

It is a good idea to close down inactive accounts because, even when inactive, they still do have an impact on your overall potential debt exposure. You also do not want to have to pay annual fees for absolutely nothing, or risk damaging your credit score because you have annual fees accruing and going unpaid when you did not know about them.

Manage Your Credit Limits

One useful trick, and one I advocate only if you have firm discipline is to accept credit limit increases on your remaining accounts, within reason. Whilst your overall credit exposure is a factor, maintaining your cards balances at no more than 30% of your limits has a much more positive impact on your credit rating.

You might find that as your credit rating improves, you are offered credit increases. If this will put you closer to only using 30% of your limit, and if it is NOT going to increase your spending, this can be a quick and easy way to improve your credit rating.

If, however, you are concerned that you may max these cards out in a moment of weakness, skip this step altogether.

Chapter 20: Student Loan Forgiveness

There are certain circumstances might lead to your loans being forgiven, canceled, or discharged. A student may qualify for these programs under certain requirements are met.

Closed School Discharge-is when your school closes while you're enrolled or soon after you withdraw, you may be eligible for discharge of your federal student loan. (For **Direct Loans, Federal Family Education Loan (FFEL) and Perkins Loans**)

Death Discharge- if the borrower, parent PLUS loan borrower die, then your federal student loans will be discharged. If you are a parent PLUS loan borrower, then the loan may be discharged if you die, or if the student on whose behalf you obtained the loan dies. (For **Direct Loans, Federal Family Education Loan (FFEL) and Perkins Loans)**

Discharge in Bankruptcy (in rare cases) you must prove to the bankruptcy court that repaying your student loan would cause undue hardship. (For **Direct Loans, Federal Family Education Loan (FFEL) and Perkins Loans).**

Total and Permanent Disability (TPD) Discharge- A TPD Discharge can be granted on the basis of your total and permanent disability. If you are a veteran that is totally and permanently disabled from a service-connected injury, you can submit documentation from the U.S. Department of Veterans Affairs showing determined that you are unemployable you can receive loan forgiveness. If you are receiving Social Security Disability Insurance (SSDI) or Supplemental Security Income (SSI) benefits, you can submit notice of award for SSDI or SSI benefits stating that your next scheduled disability review will be within five to seven years also a written certification from a physician, that you are totally and permanently disabled and unable to substantial gainful activity by this medical reason. . (For **Direct Loans, Federal Family Education Loan (FFEL) and Perkins Loans).**

171

False Certification of Student Eligibility or Unauthorized Payment Discharge- Direct Loan or FFEL Program loan can be discharge in circumstances in which your loan was falsely certified because you were a victim of identity theft or school certified your eligibility, but because of a physical or mental condition, age, criminal record, or other reason you are disqualified from employment in the occupation in which you were being trained. In cases school signed your name on the application or promissory note without your authorization or the school endorsed your loan check or signed your authorization for electronic funds transfer without your knowledge, unless the proceeds of the loan were delivered to you or applied to charges owed by you to the school. (For **Direct Loans and Federal Family Education Loan (FFEL)).**

Perkins Loan Cancellation and Discharge- Individuals who volunteer in the Peace Corps ACTION program, nurse or medical technician, member of the U.S. armed forces, law enforcement or corrections officer, teacher, a Head Start worker, a Child or family services worker, and professional provider of early intervention services. In these occupations, for each complete year of service, a percentage of the loan may be canceled. The total percentage of the loan that can be canceled depends on the type of service performed. Depending on the type of loan you have, and when that loan was taken out, you may be eligible to cancel part of or your entire loan (For **Perkins Loans)**

Unpaid Refund Discharge - if you withdrew from school, but the school didn't pay a refund that it owed you may be eligible on the amount of unpaid refund. You may qualify for this partial discharge whether the school is closed or open. Contact your loan servicer for more information. (For **Direct Loans, Federal Family Education Loan (FFEL)**

Teacher Loan Forgiveness-teachers, who have been teaching full-time in a low-income elementary or secondary school or educational service agency for five consecutive years, may be able to have as much as $17,500 of your subsidized or unsubsidized loans forgiven. (For **Direct Loans and Federal Family Education Loan (FFEL)**

Public Service Loan Forgiveness- There are loan forgiveness program if you are employed in certain public service jobs and have made 120 payments on your Direct Loans the remaining balance that you owe may be forgiven. Only payments made under certain repayment plans may be counted toward the required 120 payments. You must not be in default on the loans that are forgiven. (For **Direct Loans)**

Student Loan Forgiveness At The End Of The Term- Income Contingent, Income Based, or Pay As You Earn repayment plans offers loan forgiveness at the end of your term if you still have a remaining balance. Depending on the repayment plan you chose of 20-25 years, when your loans were your loans were borrowed originally. The amount forgiven is based on the original loan amount, your earnings, and earnings fluctuations during your repayment term.

Chapter 21: Negotiate With Your

Creditors

Contrary to common belief, your lenders and creditors are not your enemies. Your lenders act the way they do because the nature of their business dictates them to strive on profits. When you do not pay your bill, it impacts your creditor's ability to do business. However, many lenders are willing to understand your difficult financial situation, especially if you are ready to openly communicate with them efficiently and in a timely manner.

In other words, instead of missing a handful of payments or defaulting on loan, make a point to contact your creditors and negotiate with them to give you some solution, so that you can come out of your debt and increase your credit score.

What options do I have when negotiating with my lenders and creditors?

If you are under financial stress and want to boost your credit score within a month, the only option that you have is to contact your creditors and negotiate your terms. There are a wide range of options before you when you negotiate. You can go forward with options like:

☐ Lowering your monthly payments

☐ Take away one or more payments

☐ Waive off penalties and fees

☐ Lower down your interest rate

☐ Restructure your entire loan such that it makes it more achievable

☐ Create a long term payment plan

☐ Settle the account for up to 50% less than the original amount

TOP tips that will help you negotiate with your creditor:

☐ If you are denied a request for any reason, asks to speak with their supervisor

☐ Before negotiating, know your financial situation well, so that you do not agree to pay more than you can actually afford

☐While you are in between your negotiation process, figure out the extent to which your lender is willing to do a settlement and mold your strategies accordingly. Paying anywhere between 50% and 70% of the total amount, either as a full lump sum or with the help of a payment plan, is not that bad.

☐Try your best not to be afraid of the person with whom you are negotiating, even if they make threats of suing you.

☐Always remember that successful negotiators require several rounds of counteroffers and offers to come to a final settlement. This could take weeks.

☐Your lender is a trained professional when it comes to debt and may use legal terminology during a conversation to intimidate you. Do not be afraid, but listen carefully to him and understand exactly what you are committing to. You can take the help of a lawyer or a counselor if you have any questions

Chapter 22: Identitytheftand Your Credit

You have most likely heard everything there is to know about identity theft and how it can destroy your credit. But what many people do not realize is that there are ways to overcome this type of crime and regain good standing with their credit. This is done by using professional credit repair services.

By now you most likely know how to prevent identity theft. Still, despite all efforts, thieves continue to come up with different ways to steal the identity of someone who has good credit. With each preventative method that is discovered, the ID thieves come up with a new approach to carry out their nefarious plans.

If you find out that you have been the victim of identity theft, you should get copies of your credit reports right away. You can see what damage has been done. You should also inform them that you have been the victim of this crime so that they can flag your accounts. This will prevent any new accounts from being opened in your name. This can be a hassle for you but will stop any further activity from occurring.

You will then need to file an affidavit stating that the debt accrued due to the theft is not from you. You will have to sign the affidavit, have it notarized and then send it to the credit bureau. You may have to do this on more than one account. In some cases, the lender will want an affidavit with a signature guarantee, which is a little bit more reliable than just a notary. You can usually get this service at your local bank. Some people report that they have a difficult time removing items that are not theirs from their credit reports and would rather hire a company to do this. You can use a credit repair service to remove errant items from your credit reports, although you will still have to sign some forms. If you have a difficult time reading a credit report, you might also want to consider using a service for this matter. It may be more effective than trying to perform this task yourself as it can end up costing you a great deal of time and at times can also be very frustrating.

Identity theft can really wreck your credit, but it does not have to. By using preventative measures, taking stock of your credit and using a credit rewind service, you can get your credit back to where it was before the ID thieves struck.

In this day and age, one of the most common types of crimes being committed the world over is identity theft. Therefore, it is important that you protect yourself against this type of crime. Moreover, you need to know what you must do if you find that you have become a victim. Through this ebook, you are provided information about how stolen identification can impact your credit score. You are also provided with information about what you need to do in order to deal with your credit score after you have been a victim.

As an aside, you need to understand fully how crucial your credit standing is when it comes to being able to get a loan - or even a credit card. The fact is that a financial institution considering extending to you a loan of any type will first look at your score. If it does not meet a minimum level, these lenders will look no further. You also need to understand that many other businesses look at them as well before they will do business with you. This includes insurance companies and even some employers.

One of the insidious effects of being the victim of identity theft is the fact that this type of crime can do serious damage to your credit report and to your financial situation in general. Indeed, you very well may see your good rating plummet into the poor range in no time at all if you are the victim.

Therefore, when you have experienced this, you need to contact the three major reporting agencies to advise them of the situation. These reporting agencies will then put what is known as a fraud alert on your credit report. Through the placement of a fraud alert, you will be able to prevent further harm and damage to your personal financial reports.

Keep in mind that the work to correct your it is not concluded with the placement of a fraud alert. You must file an appropriate affidavit with the credit reporting agency (actually with all three reporting agencies) advising them in detail of the situation and that there is erroneous data on your report that needs to be changed and corrected.

Chapter 23: The Dispute Process: What You Need To Know

Even if you know that you can repair your credit, don't just jump into it without coming up with a strategy. The first thing you should do is to list all the accounts you intend to dispute then follow with sending dispute letters for each of the accounts. You can use any of the three methods:

#Send the dispute letters through email

#Visit the individual credit bureau's office then file the dispute

#File the dispute online

After filing the dispute, it should take about 30-45 days for your dispute to be processed. This makes it critical to have the credit monitoring service to know whether the change has been made. After the time has lapsed, you should expect the next report to have such words like remains, deleted, verified, and updated. If the response isn't satisfactory, go ahead to file a new dispute.

I already mentioned that the last payment date has a significant effect (negative) on your score given that it determines the period within which an entry shows in your credit report.

Don't aim to have zero balances for accounts that you settle. Instead, you should have them removed completely because a zero balance taints your rating. This zero balance will show in your report for 7 years or more; it speaks that creditors should take caution when dealing with you. You don't want that! You would rather fail to pay the debt to let it expire instead of having your credit score tainted by the derogatory zero balance! As such, even if you are to go into a pay to delete arrangement with a creditor (where you agree with a creditor that you will only pay if they agree to stop reporting that entry in your credit report).

So, what should you have in your dispute letters?

#Your Last and First name (must be spelt correctly)

#Your SSN

#Your Driver's license

#Your current home address

#Your W2 form or pay stub showing your name and SSN

*Your first and last name spelt accurately

#Any other forms of identification you may have

All these MUST be correct otherwise, your dispute will be rejected. Also, ensure that each of the dispute letters has all that information. There should also be the creditors name, the account number, and account name in each letter. Look out for variations in account numbers for the same account as creditors could sometimes have different numbers for different bureaus.

Let's now talk about the dispute strategies that you can use to repair your credit.

Chapter 24: Making Things Last

I'm sure we all understand that repairing credit is not a long term solution as to why you landed yourself in this situation in the first place. Yes, you can do a nice job of patch a leaking pipe but if you don't figure out what caused the leak, new cracks are going to appear in the future. Surely, you do not want to spend the rest of your life fixing and repairing things!

The key to ensuring that you do not collect a huge trail of debt and maintain good credit record is to learn better money management skills, and knowing how to make a budget. We are talking about simple things you can do in your life that can potentially snowball into huge savings month over month.

The first step to this is to learn how to track your expenses. A large number of people do not ever track the cash inflow and outflow of their bank accounts and this is a critical step in understanding your finances. All you need to do is carry a small notebook to jot down your daily expenses (or key it into your phone) or an envelope to collect the receipts. Try to track everything and tally your expenses at the end of the month. This will help to paint a good picture of your spending habits.

Once you know where your money is going to, you'll want to eliminate unnecessary spending! To do this, arrange your spending into broad categories and assign a priority to each category. Low priority items can be things which you can seemingly live without. This may include shopping or splurging on expensive foods. Try to eliminate the lowest ranking category from your spending habits. With your new expense target in mind, you can now create a suitable budget for yourself in the coming months!

The next step after creating a budget is to stretch your dollar! This means finding ways to save money and get the most out of a dollar spent. Here are some great examples to follow:

1) Saving Energy: Saving energy can provide up to 100-200 dollars' worth of savings every month! Turn the thermostat up a few degrees in summer and down a few in the winter (Or purchase a smart thermostat, as what they are called today). Turn off the light and TV when nobody is using.

2) Coupons: Coupons are there to help you save money, so use them! Many times, coupons can help to shave many dollars off your grocery bills

3) Reduce Car Usage: Whether you realize it or not, car expenses can be quite costly if you drive regularly and clock a lot of mileage. Petrol, road tax, maintenance and parking are just some of the few ways that a car can eat into your budget. Can you use the public transport, ride a bike or carpool to work?

4) Pack Your Lunch: The average amount of money spend on lunch by a person is between $5 to $9. That is $100 to $200 per month. Packing your own lunch is a great and healthy way of slicing that cost by more than half!

5) Mortgage: If mortgage rates are favorable, it may make sense to refinance and get a lower payment! Also, it is important to know when you can stop paying for mortgage insurance. Usually, you can stop paying after you have more than 20% equity in your home.

Budgeting may not seem like fun at first sight, but it is certainly a great way to ensure that you have a firm grasp over how you are spending cash. Prudent spending is always the best way to fundamentally fix your credit history and allowing you to spend without going into debt!

Conclusion

No one who is starting out in life expects to find themselves in financial turmoil. However, for most people, it will happen at some point during our adult lives. The three-digit FICO score can have a stronger impact on our future than any other grade we get in our lives. Yet, no matter how bad it seems there is no point where it can't be turned around and improved.

The reality is that we live in a society that almost demands that we have some form of credit, not to get ahead, but simply to survive. When we are without it, we suffer in more ways than one.

Studies have shown that the average American is deep in debt and nearly 40% of them are in over their heads. This can have a negative effect in many ways. The continuous worry about opening our mail every month, the constant anxiety associated with monitoring our bank accounts, and pinching pennies can be overwhelming.

What better reason is there to start mending our financial health than this? Yes, it can be scary, unpredictable, and stressful but by applying the strategies outlined in this book, you can find your way to a successful credit repair without the additional expense of hiring services to do it for you.

There is an excellent benefit to fixing your credit yourself. Not only do you save yourself from an additional expense when you are already financially strapped, but you become an expert and play a major starring role in your own life.

Learning what it takes to build your score will help you to appreciate the effort it takes to repair it. Once you've gone through these steps, you will be less likely to neglect your credit again by letting it slip back into disrepair. Through these pages you have learned:

What a credit report really is

How to read one

How your credit score is determined

How to remove errors from your account

What to do with those legitimate negative marks

How to rebuild your credit

Details about bankruptcy and how to decide if it is the right choice for you

And how to establish new credit and manage it the correct way right from the beginning.

We hope that this book has been beneficial to you and will be something you will refer to over and over again over the years. Come back to it often when you have questions but don't stop there. The more you know about credit, the easier it will be to manage your score and keep it high even when you are facing difficult times.

Once you've earned your good reputation back, work at it diligently, so you never have to struggle with the anxieties that come from poor credit management.

www.ingramcontent.com/pod-product-compliance
Lightning Source LLC
Chambersburg PA
CBHW071214210326
41597CB00016B/1807